Writing
for
Technical
Professionals

Dianna Booher
Tom H. Hill

WILEY

JOHN WILEY & SONS

New York ● Chichester ● Brisbane ● Toronto ● Singapore

Library of Congress Cataloging in Publication Data:

Booher, Dianna Daniels.
    Writing for technical professionals / Dianna Booher and Tom H.
Hill.
        p. cm.
    Bibliography: p.
    ISBN 0-471-60251-5
    1. Technical writing. I. Hill, Tom H. II. Title.
    T11.B635 1989   88-27606
    808'.0666—dc19   CIP
                                                                 AC

Printed in the United States of America

10 9 8 7 6 5 4 3 2

For
Vernon, Chris, and Lianne

How to Use This Book

Our assumption is this: You're not reading this book for entertainment. That is, you're not planning to sit down on a long Saturday afternoon with a beer and read this tome from cover to cover as if it were a spy thriller. Therefore, we've designed the book as a reference tool to be read section by section when you have a pressing problem or unanswered question. In fact, the book is a user's manual with practical how to's, not theory, as its main focus.

To overview the entire writing process in chronological steps, refer to the **Introduction.** These sequential steps will be your framework for any technical writing task. Then, to get more specific information on each step, along with examples, refer to the other parts of the book as necessary. The numerous informative headings should allow you to find the exact answers to your specific questions.

Part 1 will fill in the details on planning your document, whether it be a user's manual for a new software program or a proposal for an anticorrosion system. You'll learn time management for collecting data, audience analysis techniques, and various outlining methods.

Part 2 will take you through the drafting and revising stages of writing. You'll focus on those "Which comes first—the chicken or the egg?" dilemmas that often arise in trying to arrange your information so it has the impact you want. You'll learn effective techniques to structure paragraphs and sentences, as well as ways to add emphasis. Using these techniques will make your writing persuasive and authoritative.

Part 3 becomes more specific, with guidelines for documents such as these:

- Formal reports
- Transmittals
- Status reports
- Service and inspection reports
- Specifications
- Procedures and operating instructions
- Proposals
- Manuals
- Correspondence
- Articles in professional journals

Part 4 devotes attention to selecting and designing effective visuals.

The guidelines in **Part 5** will help put an end to the edit-rewrite-edit-rewrite syndrome experienced by managers and technical professionals within most organizations.

Finally, the **Appendixes** will answer very specific questions about matters of style concerning abbreviations, acronyms, apostrophes, hyphenation, and capitalization.

One last tip: Be sure to read the examples provided throughout to illustrate the key points. Yes, you can get the meat of all the concepts by skimming, but the examples will almost ensure that you apply the concepts correctly to your own writing.

Acknowledgments

This book came into existence primarily through the help of participants in our technical writing workshops. They asked the right questions, told us numerous anecdotes to reinforce our points, and provided us with excellent examples to illustrate the differences between effective and poor technical writing.

Specifically, we want to thank participants from client organizations such as IBM, Hewlett-Packard, Exxon, Mobil Oil, Conoco, Shell Oil, Tenneco, Pennzoil, Enron, United Gas Pipeline, and NASA, among others.

Finally, many thanks go to Chris O'Shea for her help in preparing the manuscript, catching "glitches," and generally tying up the loose ends in the publishing process.

Writing
for
Technical
Professionals

Contents

List of Figures

Introduction
Sequential Steps
in Preparing a Document

Analyzing the Audience

Everyone knows that the first step in writing is to decide who your readers are and what your purpose is. But applying that basic truth to specific writing tasks takes time. Audience analysis involves

- narrowing your purpose
- meeting the needs of both primary and secondary readers
- determining the readers' backgrounds, biases, and uses for your document.

Gathering Information and Planning the Writing While You're Doing the Work

Writing is a task to be planned and managed, just like any other work project. As the writer in charge of the final document, you are responsible for seeing that deadlines are met and that group efforts lead to a unified finished product. Managing the writing process involves

- determining deadlines for yourself
- directing group efforts
- initiating any follow-up calls or letters to see that the work is properly completed on schedule and within budget.

Organizing Your Thoughts

Difficulty in understanding technical material is more often the result of poor organization of ideas rather than the complexity of the subject. Writers try to put their thoughts on paper before they fully understand them.

Therefore, improving technical writing often involves improving the way one thinks. The late C. C. Brown, an inventor and the founder of Brown Oil Tools, held several hundred patents. He was one of the pioneers of pressure-energized seals, which work by using the pressure being contained to force a tighter seal. He often stated this basic engineering principle to younger people: Find out what's working against you, then make it work for you.

Most thoughts come to consciousness in random order, and this is fine. However, as a writer, you have to make this thought process work *for* you rather than against you. Creative people know better than to stifle thoughts while they're flowing. Don't worry if they're illogical or out of sequence. Instead, learn to catch them as they flow— by using random lists or branching methods (explained in **Chapter 3**). These thought-organizing methods can later help to generate useful outlines that serve several purposes, such as the following:

- Telling you what data you need to gather
- Revealing missing or incomplete information
- Maintaining continuity through interruptions
- Dictating schedules and deadlines
- Helping you conduct meetings
- Coordinating the work of co-writers
- Preparing progress reports

Organizing Your Document

An outline is to an effective document what a blueprint is to a house. But organizing your *thoughts* can be an entirely different process from organizing your *document*. Once you have captured all the details and data to be included, you will design the final document. That is, you will take the information and arrange it in any of several ways for the desired effect.

You don't necessarily have to write the information in the same order you think through it. Once you have a handle on your purpose, your key points, and your details, you begin to make decisions about the document's design. You may arrange your information in several

possible frameworks: most important to least important, chronological, geographical, question and answer, problem and solution, cause
and effect, comparison and contrast.

Depending on the goals you want to achieve, you can present
some ideas more effectively in one way than another.

Writing a First Draft

Writers can't afford to wait for inspiration. We've all learned the tricks
of procrastination: waiting to use the computer, clearing off the desk,
waiting to get the last test results, waiting to talk to one more expert,
organizing the files one more time, buying a new printer ribbon,
opening the morning's mail, phoning mother about her gardening,
phoning editors to see if they'd be interested in turning the report
into an article—if and when it's finished. Anything but writing.

Sooner or later, however, you have to sit down to write. Pencil
and legal pad, dictation, typewriter, or computer—whichever method
you choose must work for *you*. By that we mean that you should select
a method you can stay with over the long haul, a method that's fast
and lets you see where you've been. You can't write half a report on
the office computer and then try to write intermittently at home
without a computer. You can't dictate for hours and hours if you often
find it necessary to refer to what you've already said before you're
able to continue to the next idea. And needless to say, writing a 200-
page report by longhand would be an arduous chore. The method
must be practical, fast, and efficient.

Once you choose the method that works best for you, try to write
the entire document in one sitting, if possible. The uninterrupted effort
will bring speed, coherence, and continuity to the overall project.

Completing a first draft is 75 percent of the effort. What's left is
challenging but fun.

Editing and Revising

Hemingway had a problem with *A Farewell to Arms*; he rewrote the
ending 39 times. Soon after the novel was published, a reporter asked
him this question about his revision efforts: "What created such difficulty? What was the problem?"

Hemingway answered, "Getting the words right."

Professional writers rarely get the words right on the first try.
Neither will you. Therefore, you should allow time in your writing
schedule for revision. Most documents need attention in these areas:

- Paragraph structure
- Sentence structure
- Word choice
- Technical accuracy
- Layout and visual effects

The readability of your final document depends on

- your understanding of the subject
- the organization of the information
- layout devices such as headings, lists, margins, and adequate white space
- visuals
- coherent sentences and paragraphs
- precise words.

The last four of these items will warrant consideration during the revision stage of the writing process.

Effective technical writing is not a sprint; it's a marathon.

Writing
for
Technical
Professionals

Part 1

Planning the Document

1

Analyzing the Audience

> *Determine your objective in writing: to inform or to persuade. If you have both primary and secondary readers, assess their interest in what you have to say and their probable reactions.*

"The boss told me to" is not an objective. If the boss told you to, what is his or her objective for your report?

Some technical writers echo the famous one-liner delivered by Sergeant Friday in the *Dragnet* movie and long-running TV series: "Just the facts, ma'am." They think that as long as they present the data, they have accomplished the purpose. Not so.

Technical writers occasionally do write only to inform, for example, in the case of an operating manual or a status report. But often they also must write to persuade: to motivate someone to make a decision, to believe something, to buy something, or to fund something. In fact, if you don't explain why you did your work and persuade readers of its importance, only the other experts in your field will understand the significance of the information you present. And half of *them* will have different opinions!

The backwaters of major corporations are full of engineers who thought that it was enough to "do the engineering right." But, in fact, a good engineering solution has no value unless it gets implemented. Thus, technical professionals must also sell the merits of their work; they must overcome organizational inertia and human biases. Time is short, especially in high places, and most decision makers will not make the effort to ferret out wisdom from a woodpile of facts. Quite simply, you've got to sell!

We're *not* saying you should make devious and misleading statements. We *are* saying that you must first do the work right, then present it in such a way that the reader is motivated to do what you want.

The key to determining your purpose is to determine who your primary readers will be. Some writers like to consider other technical professionals as their primary readers, simply because they are involved in the project and need to be updated on progress that may affect their own work. But, in fact, the primary readers for most technical documents, in business anyway, are higher-level decision makers. These management readers need to move ahead, stop something, change course on the action plan, or approve further study.

1.1   A Purpose Statement
Versus a Message Statement

> *A purpose statement is a prose table of contents; it describes what readers will learn if they keep reading. A*

> *message statement provides readers with the most im-*
> *portant information. You should generally prefer a mes-*
> *sage statement over a purpose statement.*

Your primary readers determine your purpose for writing. Therefore, when fine-tuning your objective, enlarge the concept to include your most important message to them.

A purpose statement says, "This report will present evidence that someone harmed one of your relatives."

A message statement says, "Marcus Snicklefritz murdered your mother."

A purpose statement:

We have had problems in delivery of the vacuum pump and porta-power at the Octobron field site. We need your approval on a decision that will affect our completion date.

A message statement:

We have been unable to get delivery of a vacuum pump and porta-power at the Octobron field site because of the vendor's manpower shortage. We need your approval to change suppliers from Abbott Fielden to Bletz International.

A purpose statement:

This report will outline several major problems that occur during the continued recycling of lithium negative electrodes.

A message statement:

Three major problems that occur during the continued recycling of lithium negative electrodes are dendritic growth, film formation on the electrode surface, and dimensional instability.[1]

Don't stop with only a purpose statement; summarize the total message in an informative message statement. Identifying your primary readers and devising your purpose and message statements

---

[1] Jeffrey W., Braithwaite, "Materials for the New Batteries," *Advanced Materials & Processes Inc. Metal Progress*, April 1987, p. 69. Reprinted by permission of the publisher.

constitute the most difficult yet the most essential part of writing. Formulate the message statement in your mind before you even attempt to draft a complete document.

1.2   Three Ways to Handle Secondary Readers

Present your information by writing separate documents to address the needs of different readers, by designing different sections for different readers, or by using the need-to-know arrangement of details.

So what about all those secondary readers, those who will read your report, proposal, or manual simply to be informed or to take assigned action rather than to make a decision? You can address their needs with one of three options, always keeping in mind not to dilute your message to Mr. Big or Ms. Powerful.

Write multiple documents.   Slant each document to meet the needs of a particular reader or group of readers. That's the logic behind most transmittal letters. The items of interest to the senior decision maker—conclusions and recommendations—appear in the cover letter. The full report then presents the details that will satisfy other technical professionals.

Design different document sections for different readers.   An informative table of contents and descriptive headings will take decision makers immediately to the executive overview or the conclusions. Geologists can go directly to "Test Results" to find details about the six contaminated samples at the well site.

Arrange ideas in the need-to-know format.   A third option to help readers find the information of most interest to them is the need-to-know arrangement. In journalism circles, this is called the *inverted pyramid*. The headline presents the most important information—the message that is of interest to all readers. Some readers will stop after that headline. Others may read the first paragraph for the who, what, when, where, why, and how details. Still other readers may stay with the story to discover all the details. This need-to-know arrangement, with the most important information up front, satisfies all readers by permitting them to control their own reading. As soon as each person's need to know is satisfied, he or she can stop.

In technical reports, we can accommodate various levels of interest in much the same way. The abstract (or executive summary) tells all readers the most important facts. Some readers may stop reading there. Those who want details continue into the body of the report or skip to a particular section.

The same need-to-know principle applies to manuals. Suppose a user wants only to install the Lotus 1-2-3 software onto a hard disk. In that case, she can stop reading after the installation procedures. If the user wants to learn how to do only one budgeting procedure, she refers only to the appropriate section of the manual. On the other hand, if the user wants to learn the entire spreadsheet package, she continues through each section.

1.3   Determining the Audience's Background

Determine if your readers are technical or nontechnical and how much they already know about your subject.

The key question regarding the background of your readers is this: How much will my readers already know about my subject? More specific questions include the following:

- Will the readers understand the significance of this research?
- Will the readers understand the technical, human, and economic implications of the conclusions?
- Will the readers understand all the jargon, acronyms, abbreviations, and symbols?

Your assessment of the readers' background knowledge will greatly influence your decisions about which details to include and which to omit, about the overall document structure, and about the tone.

1.4   Assessing the Audience's Biases

Determine if your readers' reactions will be positive, negative, or neutral. That bias will affect which details you select and how you arrange them.

Rarely do writers find unbiased readers. That is, most readers have a stake in the subject of your writing. Determining the strength of your readers' biases may be the difference between accomplishing and not accomplishing your purpose.

If, as a proposal writer, you know the client already likes your approach to the problem, it may be unnecessary to outline all the alternatives. If, on the other hand, you know the reader will react negatively to your suggestion to use weld-over sleeves and instead favors the use of a smaller-diameter pipe, then you will want to address both options. You will mention and refute other alternatives, detailing the reasons why your proposed solution is best.

If your audience is neutral, you will be as thorough and persuasive as you think necessary to move your readers from inertia into action. Can you interest them by dangling a new product possibility in front of them? Can you quantify the savings in your research plan? Can you show them what the competition may decide to do?

Reader bias always affects acceptance of ideas. Don't ignore it; instead, let that bias help determine the structure, tone, and detail of your document.

1.5 Selecting the Appropriate Forum

Your message may not need to be written at all. If it does need to be written, determine how formal the document should be.

After a thorough analysis of your audience, you have one last chance to stop the writing process—before you get started. Are you sure that your reader and purpose can best be served by a formal report? Would a meeting or phone call accomplish the same objective? Would an electronic message suit your purpose as well? Much of what we in the corporate world put in writing should never see the white of paper.

But if you determine that you really do need to write, in what form should you send your message? Will the reader need this information only once? Perhaps you could send a quick informal memo.

Will your information be used for reference over a long period of time? If so, design it with informative headings so that readers can easily skim or relocate specific information.

Will your information be used by a reader (perhaps your immediate supervisor) to persuade someone else up the line to take action? If so, include adequate detail and don't rely on past explanations of your research. Give your immediate reader all the background and explanation necessary to understand your conclusions thoroughly enough to defend them to others involved in the decision.

Will your reader distribute different parts of your information to different readers? If so, be sure each piece of information—transmittal, exhibit, attachment—is independent of the remainder of the document.

On occasion, the form the message takes may be as important as the message itself. A document that looks too perplexing to read may condemn your project to oblivion. On the other hand, an informal memo may not get proper attention.

The plan sheet in **Figure 1–1** may be helpful in analyzing your audience before you start to write.

Audience Analysis Planning Sheet

Primary readers:

My objective in writing:

My message statement to the primary readers:

Secondary readers:

Their interest in my information:

Audience background:

Primary readers:

Secondary readers:

Audience bias:

Positive, negative, or neutral? Why?

How will I deal with that bias?

Is this information for one-time use, later reference, or distribution to others? What would be the most appropriate format?

Figure 1–1. Audience analysis planning sheet. Plan your communication to meet the needs of your readers.

2

Managing Your
Preparation Time

> *Take the project management approach to writing. As the primary writer, you must take charge of information collection, deadlines, and coordination of all group writing efforts.*

A well-written report, proposal, or manual doesn't just happen; it must be planned, designed, and coordinated—in short, managed. Writing a draft is one of the later stages of the overall project, not the beginning. To begin the project effort, you need to set deadlines for yourself for each phase.

Work backward from your due date. Depending on the length of the document, of course, you should plan on several days (several weeks would be better) between completion of the first draft and revisions and completion of the final document. The interim cooling-off period between first and final drafts allows you to approach the revision stage objectively with a fresh eye.

After you've counted backward from the final due date to the first-draft deadline, continue to count days until you have set interim deadlines for all phases of your work. Your planning calendar should include deadlines for the following:

- Calls to all people supplying information
- A completed outline
- An outline-review meeting with any other writers involved and with the supervisor
- Requests for artwork
- First drafts from all writers of sections
- The compilation of a complete first draft
- Comments on the first draft from all reviewers
- An artwork review meeting
- The revision of the document
- Manuscript preparation by the typist
- Final proofing and submission

Assuming you've marked your project calendar with all these deadlines, don't count on all co-workers to automatically meet them. Make additional notes on your calendar for such things as follow-up phone calls to remind others involved of their upcoming deadlines.

As far as your own part in the writing effort, you may find useful the following tips collected from numerous professional writers.

Mull over your writing project while you are still doing the preliminary work. Don't wait until you actually begin drafting the document. Fifty percent of any writing effort is thinking. While you are performing tests or visiting clients, you can begin to analyze your audience and decide how you want to approach the writing. Your subconscious will do wonders while you are going about your other duties.

That is not to say your conscious mind shouldn't also be engaged in the writing project. You as a technician have the power to polish your technical task in order to polish your presentation.

Suppose you are an engineer conducting a test to determine the effects of a machining process on the final surface finish. You are measuring the root-mean-square smoothness of various pieces and compiling data that will form the basis of your conclusions. You will make graphs and tables to summarize and support your findings. But think how much more impact your report would have if you include photos of the surfaces using low-angle light. Such photos would give the reader a much better "feel" for the conclusions, especially if the reader doesn't speak RMS.

Who among us has not sat down to write a report only to say, "I wish I'd got that data point . . . or that photo"? How many times have you sifted through that stack of "snapshots" of your test apparatus, looking in vain for the one that shows exactly what you want to convey?

Sometimes you can redo your work. Often, however, it will be impractical to restart your experiment or test. The conditions aren't right. Money is not available. The apparatus has crumbled into dust.

As you gather and evaluate data, you begin to form conclusions. Like any good technical professional, you ask yourself, "What new data do I need to satisfy myself that this conclusion is valid?" Then you collect more data until you're satisfied. What we're suggesting is that you also, from the very beginnning of the project, ask yourself, "What photo, data point, measurement, slide, table, or other graphic will increase the value of my final written presentation?"

Keep notes. Don't ever trust your memory. As ideas come to you about points to include, facts to state, arguments to present, or artwork to use, jot them down and toss them into a file. When you get to the drafting stage, much of your outline work will come from these bits and pieces.

Plan each section of the document. If you don't have time to organize your thoughts, how will you ever have time to revise the draft once it's down on paper? And that's exactly what you'll have to do if you string your information together without forethought.

Set aside blocks of time to write.   You lose time and continuity in "getting into" a project each time you temporarily put it aside. If you cannot devote full days to the writing effort, at least faithfully devote two to three uninterrupted hours each day.

Use prime time to write, and putter around only in off-peak hours.   If you're a morning person, write the first two to three hours of your day. If you're more energetic in the afternoon, set aside a few hours then. Thinking and writing require high-energy time.

Psyche yourself out of procrastination.   Break the writing project into small sections and then do the easy parts first—perhaps write the introduction or the section on procedures or compile a list of visuals to include in the document. As your "finished" pile grows, you will gradually get over the halfway mark and become motivated to finish the more difficult parts of the writing task.

Inspiration comes only to prophets. The rest of us have to tackle writing just as we do any other project--with planning, determination, and coordinated effort.

3

Organizing Your Thoughts

The Formal Outline,
the Random List,
the Computer-Screen Outline,
and the Idea Wheel

> *Organizing your thoughts into a writing plan saves time and produces a more effective document. Choose one of four methods to organize your ideas: the formal outline, the random list, the computer-screen outline, or the idea wheel.*

Writing workshop participants frequently confess, "I was one of those students who always wrote the paper first and afterward prepared an outline to hand in." Those people, unknowingly perhaps, miss the real shortcut to writing a final document. They view the outline as a final product rather than as an effective means to an end.

Why not just write a first draft first? Two reasons: time and help. Here's how you will use your outline.

To gather your information.   An outline indicates what points you plan to cover and helps you decide what figures, tables, or artwork you will need to support each point. If you wait until you draft the report to determine what support you might need, you will be hopelessly behind schedule in your writing. You'll be forced either to omit the additional information or graphics or delay the writing. Neither is a good option.

To visualize and overview the final document design.   Just as engineers design prototypes of new products, writers benefit from seeing what the end document will look like while there's still time to alter the writing plan. With an outline in hand, you can see where the main emphasis falls in your document. Are you getting mired in minutiae? Are you devoting more time to specifications than benefits or vice versa? That is, have you spent too many words on *how* something works rather than on *why* the reader should do what you want? Have you presented an adequate survey of the published literature on the subject?

With this outline in hand, you can often avoid the need for major rewrites by asking supervisors for their comments on your writing plan. Have you covered all the key issues? Do they agree with your interpretations? Do they want to add a key point to your plan? Getting this prewriting approval on your outline will often keep you from turning in a completed report only to hear from a supervisor, "This isn't exactly what I had in mind. Now when you rewrite this. . . ."

To discover missing or incomplete information.   An outline points out deficiencies in your thinking and in your data. As you plan, you may list points to make and then realize you have no evidence or information to support them. This discovery puts you back on the data-collection trail before time runs out.

To eliminate repetition. Those who don't plan are doomed to repeat themselves needlessly. When you see overlapping ideas and details in your structure, you can make immediate decisions about where to include such information and where to eliminate it.

To set schedules and deadlines. Many people claim to work better under pressure. Often they're making a false assumption; it's only that they have no basis for comparison. For some people, every document they produce must be completed "under pressure," and they never have an opportunity to see how much more effective they could have been had they devoted the proper time to their writing.

With an outline, you have the trail in black and white before you, making it very difficult to tell yourself there's just another "hour or two" of writing to go before completion. Realism sets in. You can time yourself to see how many hours or days you need for each section of the document and plan your schedule and the interim deadlines accordingly. Bosses and other colleagues who may be involved will also appreciate receiving a realistic schedule of deadlines from you.

To maintain continuity through interruptions. An outline functions much like a bookmark. It helps you keep your place in the project through interruptions. You can break your train of thought to take a phone call—or a two-week vacation—and come back to the project without having to reread to find out what you've already written or what you were planning to say next.

To conduct meetings and work with co-writers. You'll also find it much easier to break the writing project into portions and assign them to colleagues. All those involved will know what others are doing and what structure and format they're using. The result will be a more cohesive document. When you and your colleagues meet to discuss various phases of the writing project prior to completion, a working outline will answer questions and help you anticipate and circumvent problems.

To prepare progress reports. The meat of your progress reports comes from your outline. You can skim the writing plan for data and details as they become available. The outline becomes your tickler file for reporting.

The Formal Outline

So how do you design an outline that isn't an afterthought? You have four methods available, of which the most time consuming and least effective is the formal academic outline (see **Figure 3–1**).

Formal Outline

I. Introduction—pipelines installed
   A. Trunk lines
   B. Connections from new fields to existing systems
   C. Infield lines connecting platforms to central facility

II. Problem issues
   A. Hazardous diving
   B. Difficult repairs
   C. Complex tie-ins

III. New pipelay techniques
   A. Welding techniques
      1. Friction welding
      2. Flash-butt welding
      3. Laser welding
      4. Electron-beam welding
   B. Lay-barge procedures
      1. Laying
      2. Inspection
      3. Piggybacking
   C. Tow methods
      1. Bottom tow
      2. Off-bottom tow
      3. Control-depth tow
   D. Trenching
      1. Jet sleds
      2. Plows
      3. Mechanical trenching machines

Figure 3–1. Formal outline. Such an outline can be counterpro-
ductive to the writing effort. It is useful primarily when you already
know what you want to write.

The formal outline is not a thinking tool. It is helpful only when
you already know exactly what you want to say. If you decide to use
this traditional outlining method, you can use either words and phrases
or complete sentences. If you use only words and phrases, be complete
enough so that you don't forget what point you want to make. For
example, does "torque-turn analysis" mean that you plan to tell why
such an analysis is significant or to explain the procedure for such
an analysis? Complete sentences leave a clear trail to follow when
you are writing your first draft.

The Random List

A second outlining technique is to generate a random list. That is, you don't worry about what should come first, second, third, and so on. You don't even stop to consider which are major points and which are minor points. You simply list ideas as they come to you. Then after you have the idea list in front of you, you take a pen or pencil of another color and arrange the items into some logical order (see **Figure 3–2**).

Such a random list makes use of the brain's ability to pull ideas from many sources. Putting ideas down on paper without sorting or evaluating them helps keep the ideas flowing quickly. Later, with the entire "database" captured in front of your eyes, your brain can sort and file.

The Computer-Screen Outline

The computer-screen method is an improvement on the random list method. The concept of random listing still applies, but the list is typed on a computer. The advantage is that the list can be revised and then the revised list printed, giving you a clean outline. In other words, you can do a cut-and-paste job without the cut and paste showing.

The Idea Wheel

We recommend the fourth outlining method, the idea wheel, for speed and efficiency. Other writers refer to the technique in other ways—*branching*, *brain writing*, and *clustering*, to name a few.

As with the random list method, the technique lets you capture your thoughts randomly as quickly as you can and then reorder them easily as you move along with your first draft.

Start with your key concept written inside a circle (or wheel hub) in the center of the page. As you think of ways to break down that broad concept, draw spokes from the hub. For subpoints, draw spokes on the spokes. When you see repetition, you can immediately make a decision, for example, whether to discuss a particular detail under spoke A or spoke B. Rearrange the details immediately. When you run off the page, simply turn the spoke into another wheel hub and start the process over so as to break down your ideas further. After you have captured all your ideas on the page, go back and add numbers and letters to show the logical order (see **Figure 3–3**).

Random List Outline

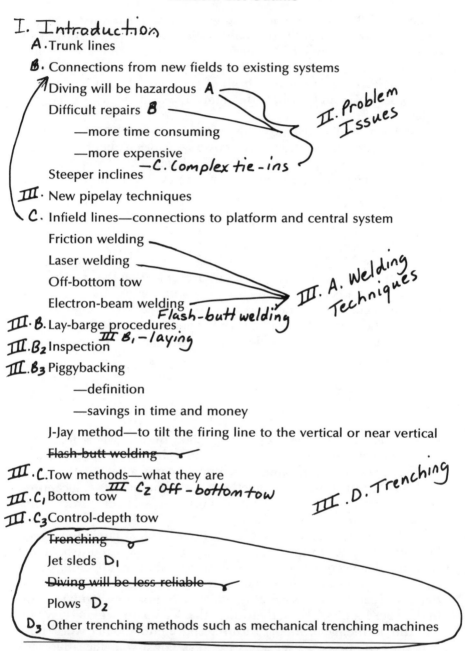

I. Introduction
A. Trunk lines

B. Connections from new fields to existing systems

Diving will be hazardous **A**

Difficult repairs **B**

—more time consuming

—more expensive

Steeper inclines —C. Complex tie-ins

II. Problem Issues

III. New pipelay techniques

C. Infield lines—connections to platform and central system

Friction welding

Laser welding

Off-bottom tow

Electron-beam welding

Flash-butt welding

III. A. Welding Techniques

III. B. Lay-barge procedures

III. B₂ Inspection   III B₁ –laying

III. B₃ Piggybacking

—definition

—savings in time and money

J-Jay method—to tilt the firing line to the vertical or near vertical

~~Flash-butt welding~~

III. C. Tow methods—what they are

III. C₁ Bottom tow   III C₂ Off-bottom tow

III. D. Trenching

III. C₃ Control-depth tow

~~Trenching~~

Jet sleds D₁

~~Diving will be less reliable~~

Plows D₂

D₃ Other trenching methods such as mechanical trenching machines

Figure 3–2. Random list outline. List all your ideas and details and then arrange them in some logical order.

18

Idea Wheels

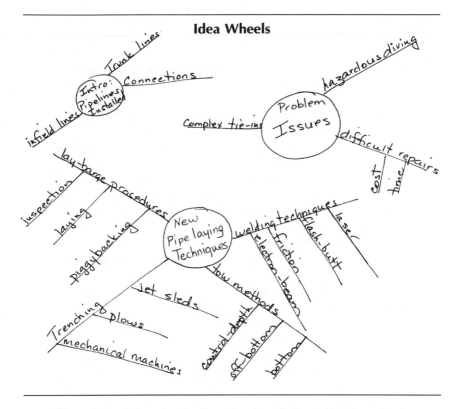

Figure 3–3. Idea wheels. Functional outlining with idea wheels helps you think and plan your document most efficiently and quickly.

In addition to outlining, technical writers have found diverse uses for this technique that have allowed them to save time and effort in the writing process.

A data-processing manager at a major oil company explains his use in this way:

> Our job is to go out in the field and interview people in different departments to find out what they do. Then we come back and write computer programs to help them do their jobs better. I used to spend one to two hours in each interview collecting data and then the other six or seven hours back in my office sorting out my interview notes to write up a memo summarizing what I'd discovered. Now I use the idea wheel in the interviewing process itself. As the interviewee talks, I take notes directly on my idea wheel. When I get back to the office, everything is already in the

right order for me to write the memo. The work's already
done.

A CFO of a financial services institution explains how he uses
the idea wheel for internal audit reports:

> In the past, we've suffered from the edit-rewrite-edit-rewrite
> syndrome around here. My two people go out to do an audit
> and then come back to the office and write their full report.
> Their supervisor reads it, makes changes, and asks for a
> rewrite. The second version goes up to the second-level
> manager, who reads it, makes changes, and asks for a re-
> write. And so on. We rewrite those reports six to eight times
> before we get them in final form.
>
> With the idea wheel, no more. The audit team simply
> captures key points on an idea wheel and then translates the
> key points to bullet points in a draft. This bullet point version,
> rather than a complete sentence draft, goes to their super-
> visor. He adds his comments and makes changes, and the
> outline goes on up the line. When the audit manager finally
> signs off on it and returns it to the audit team to draft the
> full report, he can be pretty sure the report says what he
> wants to approve. That way, we write the complete draft only
> once.

Perhaps you can think of other ways to use the idea wheel to
save time in your work. The idea wheel takes you from an idea, to
an order, to a sentence. Whichever outlining method you select, effective writing is the result of turning clear thinking into a structured
plan.

Part 2

Drafting
and Revising
Your Document

4

Organizing
Your Document

4.1 Descending Presentations

Descending presentations start with a generalization— a big-picture conclusion and recommendation—and move to the specific supportive details. The vast majority of technical reports, particularly long ones, should have a descending arrangement.

On December 9, 1941, Franklin Roosevelt addressed the nation with these opening remarks: "... So far, the news has all been bad. We have suffered a serious setback in Hawaii. Our forces in the Philippines, which include the brave people of that commonwealth, are taking punishment, but are defending themselves vigorously. The reports from Guam and Wake and Midway islands are still confused, but we must be prepared for the announcement that all these three outposts have been seized." Roosevelt then continued with the specific details.

The TV news commentator states, "The stock market plunged 508 points today. Many have lost great fortunes. Stay tuned for the details."

The newspaper journalist presents readers with this headline: "Iranian Terrorists Take 50 US Hostages." Then the specifics are given in the succeeding paragraphs.

A descending arrangement presents broad generalizations and then moves into the specifics. In a technical report, the arrangement usually looks like this:

- Summary
- Conclusions and recommendations
- Discussion
- Supplemental documentation or attachments

In a reference manual such as this book, the conclusions are set off at the beginning of each section, with elaboration of the details and supporting exhibits following.

Why this arrangement? It's direct, clear, and easy to follow. Readers can read as much—or as little—as they want. The further they move through your document, the more details they receive. If they decide to stop reading before the end of the document or the end of a section, they haven't missed any buried key points.

Most management-level technical report readers are like newspaper readers. They want capsuled information as quickly as possible because they are inundated with paperwork. Reports of all kinds— feasibility studies, research reports, statistical analyses, trip reports, marketing survey results, status reports, and investigation reports—

arrive on their desks. Needless to say, they can't read everything in full detail.

Your job as a writer is to make reading easier by presenting your most important information up front and leaving to readers how much or how little detail they want. In other words, this arrangement allows the reader to control his or her own reading according to the need-to-know principle.

Technical specialists reading your report also generally prefer this descending arrangement. Even though they may be as interested in the detailed discussion of the test procedures as in the conclusions, they will understand those details more quickly and more easily with the conclusions up front.

Compare your reactions to the two arrangements of the same material that are presented in **Figures 4–1** and **4–2**.

Descending Arrangement

Statement	Reader's Response
1. The Mark V press failure was caused by a broken blivit arm. All Mark V's have been shut down pending inspection. Full production will resume Monday, July 1.	OK.
2. Inspection procedures have been revised to prevent a recurrence of the problem.	Excellent!
3. The blivit arm failed due to metal fatigue.	I'm not surprised.
4. The fracture originated in the arm/body fillet.	Uh-huh.
5. The fillet radius was .040 of an inch smaller than design requirements.	I see why it broke.
6. Metallurgical analysis showed normal structure.	OK.
7. A complete report on the status of all blivit arms will be presented on July 10.	Good.

Figure 4–1. Descending arrangement. This arrangement of information always makes details clear and allows readers to control how much or how little elaboration they want.

4.2   Ascending Presentations
(or Why Are You Telling Me This?)

Ascending presentations begin with specifics and move to generalizations. The ascending arrangement of information can be effectively used for jokes, movies, or novels. On rare occasions, it may be useful for presenting conclusions and recommendations against which your reader is strongly biased.

The suburban housewife finishes her phone call, kisses her husband goodbye, and walks out to her car, which is parked in the garage. The garage door rises as she presses the button. From out of the shadows, a gruff voice demands that she keep her mouth shut as brutish hands claw at her throat. She gasps for breath, then slides limply to the garage floor.

Commercial. The rest of the movie finally leads to who done it.

Such is the ascending arrangement of information, the once-upon-a-time format. In a technical report, the format usually looks like the following:

- Introduction
- Scope
- Testing procedures
- Findings and discussion, with supplementary tables, figures, and charts
- Conclusions
- Recommendations

In a reference manual, the ascending arrangement might look like this:

- What's included in your software package
- Product specifications
- Steps 1, 2, 3 in performing task A
- How task A benefits the user
- Steps 1, 2, 3 in performing task B
- How task B benefits the user
- Steps 1, 2, 3 in performing task C
- How task C benefits the user

If you use this arrangement for most information, your audience must read blindfolded. You control your readers' time and attention, forcing them to follow your reasoning slowly and deliberately. If this

... then this ... then this ... therefore, it follows that .... You as the writer completely control how much or how little you want to reveal to the readers and in what order (see **Figure 4–2**).

Needless to say, the arrangement in **Figure 4–2** usually annoys busy management readers who want to control their own time. Their reaction is quite often, "Tell me what your main point is and I'll decide if I want to hear more."

On the other hand, if you think your reader is so biased against what you have to say that you have to sneak up on his or her blind side, then you might well choose the ascending format. You hold up the reader's first cherished idea, then refute it. Next, you hold up the reader's second most cherished idea, then knock it down. Finally, you present the only remaining option—your conclusions and recommendations—and hope you have left the reader no alternative but to accept your position.

Sometimes it works and sometimes it doesn't. Sometimes the reader bows to your reasoning and lets you lead him or her down the

---

Ascending Arrangement

Statement	Reader's Response
1. A complete report on the status of all blivit arms will be presented on July 10.	Why?
2. Metallurgical analysis showed normal structure.	Analysis of what? So what?
3. The fillet radius was .040 of an inch smaller than design requirements.	?
4. The fracture originated in the arm/body fillet.	Fracture? What fracture?
5. The blivit arm failed due to metal fatigue.	What blivit arm?
6. Inspection procedures have been revised to prevent a recurrence of the problem.	What problem? What procedures?
7. The Mark V press failure was caused by a broken blivit arm. All Mark V's have been shut down pending inspection. Full production will resume Monday, July 1.	*@!!**#!

Figure 4–2. Ascending arrangement. This arrangement usually exasperates a reader because details are unclear if the main message is not up front.

primrose path. On other occasions, the reader refutes your ideas each step of the way and arrives at a conclusion totally different from yours (see **Figure 4–3**).

Unless your report is so short or of such great interest that all readers will want to read every single detail, avoid the ascending arrangement.

4.3 Other Internal Structures

There are several ways to organize the details within either an ascending or a descending document format. Don't grab the first arrangement that comes to mind; choose the most appropriate one for your purpose. Whatever your choice, that organizational framework should be apparent to your reader.

To design a building, you put up the framework and scaffolding, then proceed to construct the walls. The same principle is true with writing.

One Danger of Ascending Arrangements

We're having a problem with Bill in sales.

Bill is bored with his job.

Bill's administrative assistant bungles client calls.

We could hire a new assistant for Bill, but that would not alleviate his boredom.

We could expand Bill's sales territory to challenge him more, but John would get angry.

We could increase Bill's product line to challenge him more, but the new products won't be ready for another six months.

Therefore, to motivate Bill, let's give him a bigger commission percentage [**your conclusion**].

Therefore, let's fire Bill [**reader's conclusion**].

Figure 4–3. One danger of ascending arrangements. The ascending presentation can lead to an unpleasant surprise: The reader may come to a completely different conclusion from that of the writer.

The framework is your plan for what goes where, and it should guide you in writing the document. It should also guide the reader. Much like homeowners walking along the rafters of their attic, readers should be able to see the rafters of your document and go from key point to key point without getting lost in the details between.

Some of the most widely used frameworks follow, along with some of their weaknesses.

Chronology as a framework.   Investigative reports frequently employ this structure. The arrangement moves from "once upon a time" to "they lived happily ever after." A common danger in this arrangement, however, is that writers tend to include every little insignificant detail. The choice of a chronological arrangement doesn't mean you must tell everything Tom, Dick, and Harry did. You should probably include in your chronology only important events, such as when they made good decisions, turned corners, or slid in the ditch.

Use chronological order only if the time relationships involved will contribute to the reader's understanding.

Geography as a framework.   Customer- and client-orientation documents tend to use this framework. One danger lies in repeating the structure from locale to locale. Sometimes a geographical arrangement makes sense; sometimes it doesn't.

Most important to least important as a framework.   This arrangement is commonly used in documents intended to persuade. One advantage is that it allows readers to stop reading as soon as they are convinced of your conclusions. A weakness in this arrangement is that if readers don't agree with you about which points are most convincing, you may lose them by seemingly concentrating on trivialities and ignoring what's important.

Cause to effect (or effect to a cause) as a framework.   The structure is this: Cause 1, cause 2, and cause 3 lead to effect XYZ. Or it can be stated thus: Effect XYZ is the result of causes 1, 2, and 3. A common weakness in this arrangement is that facts are presented as if they needed no interpretation. Scientists are often heard to say, "The facts speak for themselves." To this, most readers will say, "Maybe, but I don't speak that language." Thus, the writer's interpretations should bridge the gap between facts and the readers' understanding of those facts.

Comparison and contrast as a framework.   This arrangement looks like this: System A and system B are alike in X, Y, and Z. Or System A and System B differ in X, Y, and Z. Typically, a writer misuses comparison and contrast in the following manner. He or she tells us all the features and specs of machine A, then all the features and specs of machine B, and then all the features and specs of machine C. Such an arrangement is ineffective and makes it difficult to keep score— that is, readers won't know how to evaluate the facts about machine A until they have all the information about machines B and C.

If you choose the comparison and contrast arrangement, it is usually more effective to arrange the details by criteria, as shown in **Figure 4–4**. Of course, tabular presentations of criteria and options often convey information to be compared or contrasted better than paragraph arrangements (see **Part 4**).

Problem to solution as a framework. For most problem-to-solution documents, present your problem first, then the proposed solution, then supporting documentation, then refutation of alternative solutions. Omit irrelevant details.

Another possible format is to present your problem, then all the possible alternatives, knocking them down one by one. Finally, you present the solution you are proposing. This arrangement can be effective, particularly if you know your reader is against your solution.

Comparison and Contrast Documents

Ineffective	Better
Machine A	Cost
Cost	Machine A
Ease of operation	Machine B
Delivery schedule	Machine C
Machine B	Ease of operation
Cost	Machine A
Ease of operation	Machine B
Delivery schedule	Machine C
Machine C	Delivery schedule
Cost	Machine A
Ease of operation	Machine B
Delivery schedule	Machine C

Figure 4–4. Comparison and contrast documents. Arrange information by criteria, not by options.

But a big danger in saving your real conclusion (the proposed solution) until the end is that your reader may wonder where you're going and grow impatient with the irrelevant alternatives.

Description as a framework.   Descriptive passages should not consist of descriptive details jumbled together. The organization of the document should be apparent to your reader. Try to proceed from familiar ground to the less familiar or the unfamiliar.

In describing an object, generally your writing will be more effective if you describe it from the inside out. Start with the internal motor mechanism, then move outward to its casing, then to the entire vehicle body, and finally to the decorative trim.

Numerical or alphabetical arrangement as a framework.   Enumerated or alphabetized items usually indicate that all the points are equally important. The enumeration or alphabetical listing simply gives a point of reference from one document or discussion to the next.

To repeat: Your ideas will not automatically come to mind in a smooth framework. No matter. Simply use one of the organizational methods presented in **Chapter 3,** such as the idea wheel, to capture your thoughts. Then when you have all the details at hand, you can structure them into one of the document frameworks described above.

5

Paragraph Development

5.1   What Paragraphs Do for You

Paragraphs serve five major functions in your writing: to introduce, to support, to repeat, to link, to conclude.

In school, we didn't have much trouble with paragraphing because most English teachers required the standard five-paragraph essay:

- Paragraph 1: an introductory paragraph with a thesis statement
- Paragraph 2: first point and supporting detail
- Paragraph 3: second point and supporting detail
- Paragraph 4: third point and supporting detail
- Paragraph 5: conclusions and usually a restatement of thesis

Few writers ever learn the other ways paragraphs can serve them or discover the variety of paragraphs that are available. Consequently, they have monstrously long paragraphs full of details that don't really fit together well.

Think of your document as a string of chain links, not a chain-link fence. In a fence, the links (paragraphs) are rigid. But a loose chain has links that can be twisted, allowing the chain to be wrapped around whatever object you want to tie down. Your own writing should be full of twistable links—paragraphs that serve your different writing purposes.

Paragraphs can do all of the following:

Introduce an Idea

During the 1960s and 1970s, custodial care for the severely mentally ill in large state hospitals was abandoned and replaced by care in the community. Four influences lay behind this shift.
The first was . . .[1]

Define a Term

One of the most common problems seen in the oil industry is that of cement gelation. Gelation can be defined as a premature viscosification or a gel-strength buildup of the

---

[1] Excerpted from material originally appearing in Harold M. Visotsky, M.D., "The Great American Roundup." *The New England Journal of Medicine* 317 (1987): 1662. Reprinted by permission of publisher.

cement slurry. This can have important consequences in field operations and may be so severe as to cause job failure.[2]

Outline a Step or Stage

For this method, pick up a special squeeze packer with a retrievable-drillable bridge plug and run them in the hole on the bottom of the work string to within one joint of the top perforations of the production zone.

Set the bridge plug at this depth and release packer tension. Pull four strands of the tubing out of the hole. Rig up a pumping manifold to pump separately down both the tubing and annulus. Pump the well servicing fluid down the tubing with returns run to the pit through the blooie line. This should ensure that the hole is gas-pocket free. Set the packer at this depth and fill both the tubing and annulus with the well servicing fluid.

Pressure up the annulus to a maximum surface pressure numerically equivalent to 10% of the packer's depth.[3]

Present an Analogy

"Observing the instant of a molecule's creation is for a chemist what observing the Big Bang would be for an astronomer," says Ahmed Zewail of the California Institute of Technology. "Molecules form our microuniverse and it is of fundamental importance for chemists to know how atoms and molecules get together to form new molecules."[4]

Give an Example

One example of variable hazards along a pipeline route is shown in Table 1 where a submarine pipeline is subject to increased risk of damage from anchors and dropped objects in the vicinity of an offshore platform, a low risk from anchors and fishing gear along most of the subsea route, increased risk of scour from wave or current action in the near-shore

---

[2] Jacques Kieffer and Phil Rae, "How Gelation Affects Oil Well Cements," *Petroleum Engineer International*, May 1987, p. 46. Reprinted by permission of publisher.

[3] Douglas L. Patton, "How to Find Casing Leaks," *Petroleum Engineer International*, July 1987, p. 34. Reprinted by permission of publisher.

[4] Roger Lewin, "A New Window onto the Chemists' Big Bang." *Science* 238 (1987): 1512–13. Copyright © 1987 by the AAAS. Reprinted by permission of publisher.

zone, and possible third party interference on the land section.[5]

Provide a Quotation

Workers caution that whatever is found out in animals is not ipso facto transferable to humans. "Learned helplessness is one route into depression," says Steven F. Maier of the University of Colorado at Boulder. "It is not synonymous: there is no one-to-one relationship." Learned helplessness, he points out, affects every system in the brain, bringing about a potent and widespread cascade of effects that are expressed in a range of behaviors.[6]

Tell an Anecdote or Provide a Case History

Inside the refrigerated vault, a clerk at a private pediatric hospital in New York wears gloves to keep her hands warm, but when she tries to type information into the computer about the arrival and distribution of supplies, keyboard errors sometimes creep into her work because of the gloves. However, with a voice recognizer, she dictates shipment data directly into the PC—without error.

Give Reasons

The three tanks in question were sold for the following reasons: We were in the process of abandoning this lease, and had to complete land reclamation before winter. Second, the tanks had to be moved before we could reclaim the area. Third, the equipment needed to reclaim the land was already in the area, saving us time and money. Finally, to haul the tanks 200 miles to the Rewo Warehouse was economically unfeasible.

Answer a Question

What shape does the new cavity take? Because the formation sand is saturated in salt water, the cavity is probably shaped somewhat like a cone, with the angle to vertical roughly equal to the angle of internal friction for sand.

---

[5] *Pipeline Industries Guild Journal* 92 (Summer 1985): 18.
[6] "Stressed Out," *Scientific American*, November 1987, p. 30. Copyright © 1987 by Scientific American, Inc. All rights reserved. Reprinted by permission of publisher.

Provide a Solution

A difficulty that occurs with the resistance furnace is the inability to connect the power leads to the high-temperature resistance elements. This materials temperature problem is usually solved with elaborate water cooling techniques. One alternative is to feed the electrical power into the heating unit via an induction coil.

Link Two Ideas

Despite these disadvantages to the new system, the software does enhance productivity in preparing monthly statements to customers.

One advantage . . .

Restate Something Already Said

Static pressure is constant at a particular altitude above sea level and dynamic pressure varies with the square of the velocity. If one divides the total drag force by the dynamic pressure and the frontal area (pressure × area = force), the drag coefficient becomes a dimensionless parameter that *does not* depend on the frontal area of the object or its velocity. We can rearrange the drag coefficient equation thus:

$$\text{drag force} = c_d \times \text{frontal area} \times \text{dynamic pressure}$$
$$= c_d \times \text{frontal area} \times \text{constant} \times \text{velocity}^2$$

In other words, it is apparent from this equation that for a given velocity there are only two ways to reduce the drag force: Reduce the drag coefficient and/or reduce the frontal area of the object. Thus, all aerodynamic improvements to a bicycle will either reduce the drag coefficient or reduce the effective frontal area of the bicycle and rider combination.

Conclude a Point

Finally, in the atmosphere of justifiable satisfaction over the new data supporting the use of t-PA[5], it is important not to forget the knowledge gaps that remain. The optimal regimens of drug administration are unclear; the value of adjunctive therapy is not defined; and the extent of benefits and risks is incompletely known. Efforts to resolve these and related issues must continue.[7]

Most documents include a wide variety of paragraph structures. For each paragraph in **Figure 5–1**, note the structure and what the paragraph does to mold the ideas into a cohesive unit.

5.2   Overview Statements for Skimmers

Every paragraph should have an overview statement, usually the first sentence. This overview statement allows skimming readers to pick up the key points in a document and to select which paragraphs to read in full.

"You mean I'm writing all that long discussion for nothing?" workshop participants query in a hostile tone when we tell them that few readers, particularly senior executives, read every word they write in their reports.

Not "for nothing" we assure them. The long discussion of involved details and data has to be in the document to support the conclusions and recommendations. But every reader doesn't have the same interest in the same details. Therefore, most professionals will read selectively.

Overview statements or topic sentences make this selective reading possible. Therefore, be careful about using bottom-up paragraphs. Some writers give details, details, details, and then finally give the point about the details. Reverse that order. Give the reader your point, then elaborate (see **Figures 5–2** and **5–3**).

5.3   Five Ways to Make Your Paragraphs Hang Together

Paragraphs must fit together logically. Here are five techniques to give paragraphs the necessary coherence: framework devices, repetition of key words or phrases, transitional words and phrases, transitional paragraphs, and headings or lists and white space.

See if you can follow the passage on page 38.

---

[7]Excerpted from material originally appearing in Jeffrey S. Borer, "t-PA and the Principles of Drug Approval," *New England Journal of Medicine* 317 (1987): 1661. Reprinted by permission of publisher.

Various Paragraph Structures Within a Single Document

To Introduce

Egypt has maintained greater exploration and general development activity levels than most countries in the Middle East. The government's desire for new fields to sustain production has helped support activity.

To Give Statistics

In the first four months of this year, output averaged almost 890,000 b/d. For the fiscal year from July, 1987, through June, 1988, average production is forecast at 870,000 b/d.

To Give Reasons

New permits have been made available to stimulate exploration by foreign companies and a clutch of new discoveries in the Western Desert has helped maintain interest.

To Give an Example or Illustration

Development in the Western Desert has been held back by the crude oil transportation difficulties. But in the past year, two new pipelines to El Hamra terminal on the Mediterranean coast have been commissioned.

To Explain

There are now three crude pipelines spanning the desert, and a number of small finds can be linked into the transportation system.

To Link Two Ideas

While the Western Desert captures the headlines because of recent discoveries and bid rounds, the bulk of Egypt's production comes from the Gulf of Suez.

To Give Statistics

Production, principally from the El Morgan, July, and October fields (all in the Gulf), has been averaging around 500,000 b/d of oil, with 100 MMcfd of gas from the Western Desert. GUPCO accounts for just under 60% of total national output.

To Conclude

Cumulative production from El Morgan is expected to top 1 billion bbl next month.

Source: "New Pipelines in Egypt's Western Desert Spur Exploration Activity in That Area," *Oil and Gas Journal*, August 24, 1987, pp. 33–34. Reprinted by permission of publisher.

Figure 5–1. Various paragraph structures within a single document. Paragraphs can serve a variety of functions.

His lips twisted into a distorted position as he yanked the stocking and football helmet over his head. Rearranging the boxes of paperbacks in front of him, he rooted out a seat behind the door and beneath the shelving. After a moment, he stood up again, dug a knife out of his jeans pocket, examined it carefully, then tucked it into his waistband. He slid back down into the cramped space.

Danielle Ryggs returned the last composition, steeled herself against the rumblings throughout the classroom, and backed away toward her desk. She raised her eyebrows slightly to invite questions.

Overview Statements

overview Several lines of evidence indicate that the activities localized at the anterior and posterior egg poles are necessary and sufficient for the establishment of polarity in the *Drosophila* embryo. The inhibitory interactions between the anterior and posterior activities observed in the transplantation experiments may play a stabilizing role in normal development. Elimination of the anterior activity in *bcd⁻* embryos facilitates the formation of a bipolar pattern—a bicaudal embryo—in transplantation experiments. Likewise, double-headed embryos can be induced by transplanting anterior cytoplasm to the posterior of a mutant of the posterior class. In double mutants of *bicoid* and *oskar*, polarity is no longer detectable, and in transplantation experiments, head structures can be induced at the posterior end and abdomens at the anterior without encountering inhibitory effects residing in the recipient embryo. . . .

overview Although formally the two activities appear to have symmetrical (reciprocal) properties, there are a number of significant differences between the anterior and posterior activities. . . .

overview The differences between the two activities are not restricted to the degree of mutual inhibition. . . .

Source: Christiane Nusslein-Volhard et al., "Determination of Anteroposterior Polarity in *Drosophila*," *Science*, vol. 238, p. 1680. Copyright© 1987 by the AAAS. Reprinted by permission of publisher.

Figure 5–2. Overview statements. A skimming reader can read first sentences in paragraphs such as these and have the most important ideas.

Do you know what's happening? Not yet. But with a little transitional phrase such as *Further down the hallway* inserted at the beginning of the second paragraph, we would immediately understand the connection between the helmeted football player and his victim, the classroom teacher. The light goes on: Danger lurks behind the door.

Suspense is fine for the entertainment industry, but technical readers like to know where they are at all times, and you as a

---

Buried Key Ideas

Table I summarizes the oil production values of each well in the pilot area, which are illustrated in graphs 7 to 27. The best-fitting line through the oil production curve is also drawn on each graph. It is noted that 18 wells and 86 percent of the total number of producers showed an increase in oil production. This gain in oil is most significant for the five producers (13–2, 15–2, 3–11, 5–11, and 7–11) that are surrounded by four of the five treated injectors (11–2, 16–3, 1–11, and 11–11). The well 7–14–6–12, suspended in October 1970 for economic reasons, was put back on production four months after the treatment and is now producing an average of 25 BOPD at 70 percent oil cut. The total gain in oil at the end of August has been approximately 237 BOPD. It was noted that the index of determination of the individual well best-fitting lines is generally very poor (ranging from a low of .001 to .76) and only modest confidence can be placed in these results; however, the best-fitting lines through the test oil production data of the entire pilot area is characterized by good correlations (.86 and .93) and can be used with confidence. This group relationship indicates a total oil gain at the end of August of approximately 253 BOPD. This gain in oil is also confirmed by the best fitting line through the oil cut curve of the pilot area. At the bottom of Table I, the comparison can be made for each indicated date between the total derived from individual well performance and the total of the pilot area. There is good correlation between these figures.

Figure 5–3. Buried key ideas. A skimming reader might miss key points buried within a long paragraph such as this one.

writer must provide that sense of security through paragraph coherence.

Framework Devices as Transitions

The first technique, the one used in the previous excerpt, is a framework device. In other words, with those words *Further down the hallway* the reader makes the connection of place. The people are
dangerously near each other.

The most frequent framework technique is the old *first, second,
third,* and *finally* linking of ideas. Other common framework transitions include the following:

- Reasons: The first reason . . . Another reason . . . A final reason . . .
- Parts of a whole: The internal mechanism contains . . . The
  external mechanism contains . . .
- Spatial arrangement: The lower lever serves to . . . The upper
  lever serves to . . .
- Steps, stages, or processes: The boil-down stage . . . The coating stage . . .

You have the idea. The opening words of each paragraph remind
you of the document framework so that you see where each major
section starts and stops.

Transitional Words and Phrases

A second way to make your paragraphs coherent is to use transitional
words and phrases that exist as links wherever they appear in a
document (see **Figure 5–4**).

Transitions tell readers to go forward to the next point, to back
up and review where they've been, or to pause for an illustration.
Without these road signs to guide them through the details, readers
frequently lose the trail of logic from sentence to sentence or paragraph to paragraph. Note how the transitions in the following passage
provide a trail:

> Hazard analysis includes **but is more than** just a prediction
> of the consequences of failure in terms of injury to people
> or damage to property. **Although** these are not trivial **and** they
> involve the use of mathematical modelling techniques and
> engineering judgment, the analysis **also** involves identifica-
> tion of potential hazards. Such identification **then** can lead
> to recommendations for prevention.

A **second** important point, if obvious, is that the analysis must be designed to answer the particular needs of the constructor, operator, or regulatory authority who requires the study. **For example,** the study should **also** use appropriate techniques for the physical characteristics of the equipment, **both** its housing and its operating environment. **Therefore,** different approaches and methods of presenting results have to be used.

Repetition of Key Words and Phrases

The most common transition between thoughts is the simple repetition of a key idea or phrase. You can repeat exactly the same noun, give a synonym for that noun, or use a pronoun that refers to that noun.

When the meter is taken out of service, the installer should bypass the meter and close the upstream and downstream **valves**. These valves [repetition] isolate the meter from line pressure. This **procedure** [synonym] is standard in field testing because **it** [pronoun] allows quick and safe removal of the meter.

Transitions	
Therefore	Although
In addition to	So
Furthermore	For this purpose
Most of all	Accordingly
Above all	Thus
In like manner	This being true
Likewise	To illustrate
Equally	For example
But	In summary
Nevertheless	To repeat
Granted	In addition

Figure 5–4. Transitions. These words and many others like them serve as road signs.

Transitional Paragraphs

In addition to the techniques already mentioned, sometimes paragraphs need something bigger to link them with other paragraphs. In other words, the reader has been stepping from one tiny flagstone to another along the walkway, then suddenly comes to a swinging bridge over a creek. The transitional paragraph ties the two walkways together via a transitional idea. **Figure 5–5** shows how such paragraphs bridge the gap.

Headings, Listings, and White Space

Another useful transitional technique is the use of headings, listings, and white space. Each of these devices indicates to a reader the relationship of one idea to another. A new heading and surrounding white space says to the reader, "I'm finished with that idea; let's move to the next one." A numbered or bulleted list says, "This idea can be broken down into subparts." Extra white space says to the reader, "End of current topic; take a breath. Here comes a new part."

Use whichever transitional technique is most appropriate for your sentence, paragraph, or document. Just remember to leave a trail with transitions so your reader can easily follow your reasoning from point A to point B.

5.4   What to Do with "Stray" Ideas

Stray ideas easily get lost in unrelated paragraphs. When details don't seem to fit in any particular paragraph, use a miscellaneous "dumping" paragraph and alert the reader to what's there by a warning note or an all-purpose topic sentence.

You've probably seen an interior decorator cart a green plant around from place to place in a living room, backing off to take a critical look from each perspective. Writers have a similar difficulty; some details seem to defy logical placement.

When that is the case, question whether you need the detail at all. If the answer is yes, then you have two ways to call the reader's attention to it.

Transitional Paragraphs

The interior coating . . .

The exterior coating . . .

The coating on the peripheral equipment . . .

Another concern for our chemists, in addition to the coatings used, is the time required for the testing. The time requirement will create several problems in the manufacturing process.

The first timing problem is . . .

An additional timing problem is . . .

Finally, timing can be a problem when . . .

Therefore, our hesitancy in agreeing to this proposal . . . both the coating materials and the time-consuming, repeated testing required in the manufacturing process. Additionally, our management is concerned with the up-front cost for this venture.

The materials cost . . .

The cost of having on-site staff during all phases . . .

And finally, the ongoing cost of maintenance on . . .

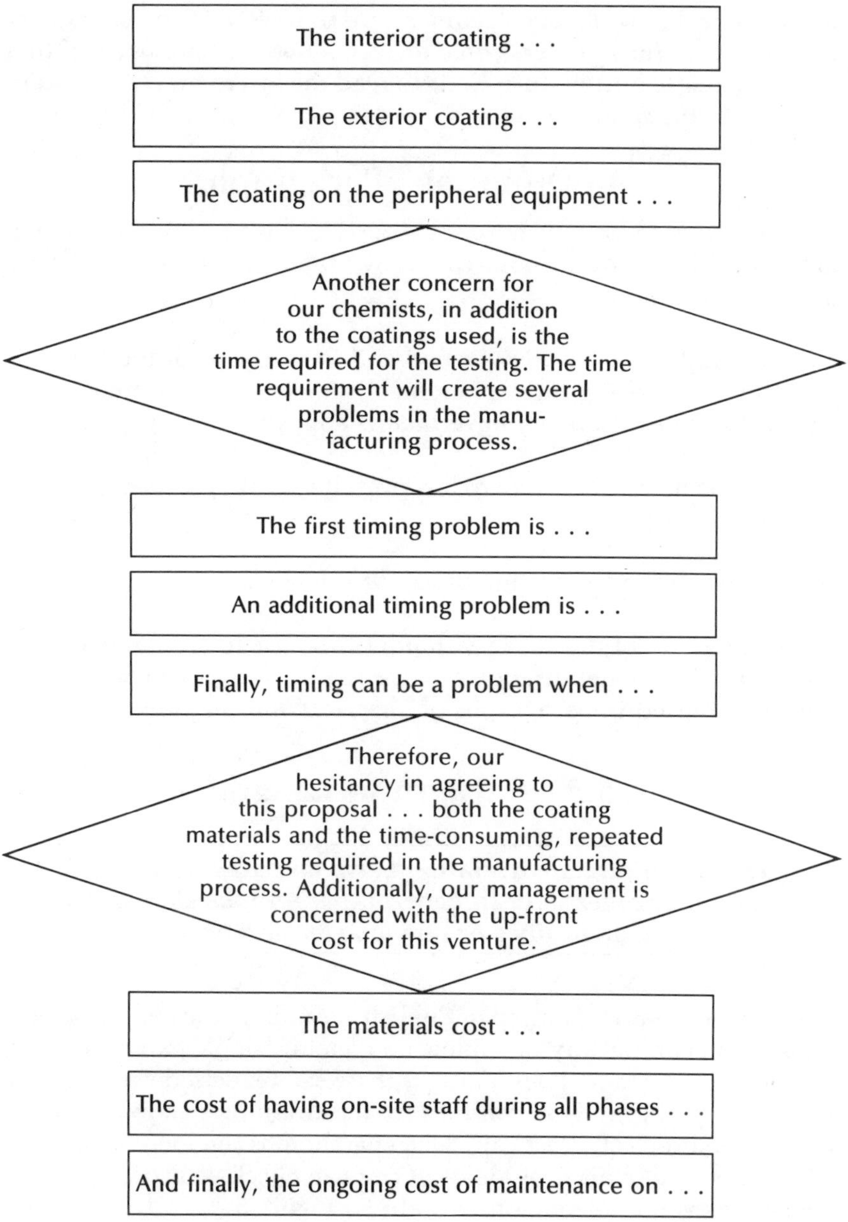

Figure 5–5. Transitional paragraphs. Such paragraphs bridge the gaps between major sections of the document.

A Warning Note

First, when some fact, statistic, qualifier, or other explanation doesn't fit the logical flow of your document, mark it **NOTE:** and change the page layout. When readers come to such a note, it's almost as if they press the pause button, turn aside to read the insert, and then resume the flow of the main ideas.

A "Dumping" Paragraph

A second way to present miscellaneous ideas is in a "dumping" paragraph with an all-purpose overview statement. Consider the examples that follow:

> In addition to the slow speed and imprecision of the machine, there are other minor inconveniences, inconsequential to most users but nevertheless annoying: . . .

> Let me insert one caution, however, before we proceed with the other steps: . . .

> Other secondary testing procedures included . . .

Whichever of the above techniques you use to present necessary but hard-to-place details, don't let the reader overlook them by keeping them buried in paragraphs of unrelated information.

5.5   Paragraph Length

There is a direct correlation between paragraph length and comprehension. In general, paragraphs should not exceed about 14 lines or one-quarter of a page.

Contrary to what we learned in English class about the five-paragraph theme, you can't always complete an idea in a single paragraph. Eye appeal is important. Long paragraphs wear readers down, particularly long paragraphs of complex material. Studies show that comprehension drops off drastically when paragraphs run more than about 14 lines or one-quarter of a page. (You can check your own comprehension as you read versions 1 and 2 in **Figure 5–6**.)

There is no minimum length for a paragraph. A transitional paragraph may be only one word (often used for effect in fiction) or one sentence.

Paragraphing: Comprehension and Eye Appeal

Version 1:

These sound waves are analyzed by the instrument and the results are displayed on the CRT as wave forms. There are four characteristic wave forms. The patterns are easy to identify and remember: The ideal weld displays a short, double-spaced train because the sound wave has penetrated both mating pieces. The returning sound shows a decrease in intensity and amplitude. A second pattern occurs when no weld is formed. The echo train is tall and single-spaced, indicating that only one piece of sheet metal has been penetrated. Attenuation is low because there is no weld nugget to absorb the sound. Still another pattern is revealed by a marginally undersized weld. Single spacing appears between double-spaced echoes because only a portion of the sound has penetrated the weld. The rest has been reflected from the mating surface. The last pattern is that of a stick weld. The echo train is double-spaced, but it is tall because no sound attenuation has occurred—even though both pieces of metal have been penetrated.

Version 2:

These sound waves are analyzed by the instrument and the results are displayed on the CRT as wave forms. There are four characteristic wave forms. The patterns are easy to identify and remember:

- *Ideal weld.*   The echo train is short and double-spaced because the sound wave has penetrated both mating pieces. The returning sound shows a decrease in intensity and amplitude.

- *No weld formed.*   The echo train is tall and single-spaced, indicating that only one piece of sheet metal has been penetrated. Attenuation is low because there is no weld nugget to absorb the sound.

- *Marginally undersized weld.*   Single spacing appears between double-spaced echoes because only a portion of the sound has penetrated the weld. The rest has been reflected from the mating surface.

- *Stick weld.*   The echo train is double-spaced, but it is tall because no sound attentuation has occurred—even though both pieces of metal have been penetrated.

(Version 2 is reprinted with permission from Tony Midora, "On the Spot Testing of Welds," *Mechanical Engineering*, September 1987, p. 77)

Figure 5–6.   Paragraphing: comprehension and eye appeal. The long paragraph in version I makes the information difficult to read and to recall. Version 2, with smaller paragraphs and informative headings, is more appealing to read and easier to retain.

Transitional words and phrases will lead your reader into a new paragraph even if the subject of the previous paragraph is not fully developed. Perhaps one paragraph presents three reasons for some course of action. With a good transitional phrase such as *a fourth reason,* the reader will continue into the new paragraph for the rest of the idea.

Every time readers come to a new paragraph in the text, they can pause, take a deep breath, and tackle a new idea. A paragraph is the pause that refreshes.

6

Sentence Structure

6.1   The Long and Short of It: Sentence Length Sets Reader Pace

Sentences should be as long or as short as necessary to serve your purpose. The average sentence should not run more than about 20–25 words. Both sentence length and pattern determine the reader's pace through your material.

When one engineer we know went to work for a large corporation, his boss told him that no sentence should be longer than 26 words. For over 20 years, this man has dutifully counted every word in sentences approaching this limit. He still feels guilty: "Should articles also count as words? This sentence has 29, but I can't think how to rewrite it."

The *average* sentence length in business and technical writing today is about 20–25 words. But the issue should always be clarity, not obedience to artificial restraints. Occasionally, however, technical writers will run a sentence marathon in which they try to convey every known detail and qualification about a concept in a single sentence. Consider the following example:

> By increasing the trapped-gas saturation alone, the relative permeability to water is reduced to be consistent with the relative permeability relationship measured in the lab; however, the physical system is more nearly represented by parallel flow paths for the gas and water phases so that the water relative permeability at the increased trapped-gas saturation should be increased to the conformance fraction of the water relative permeability at the original trapped-gas saturation. [74 words]

Technical information is complex enough for most readers without the writer making it more difficult with complicated sentence structure. The longer the sentence, the more decoding effort is required to get to the basic idea.

Consider these paraphrased clichés:

> A miniscule amount of effort to avert undesirable occurrences is the equivalent of a much greater countermeasure.

> When one comes to a point in one's life at which one experiences an overwhelming desire to pursue and achieve a specific goal, one's mental faculties, creativity, and emo-

tional strength will overcome all obstacles standing between one and the desired goal.

Did you recognize the clichés? How about "An ounce of prevention is worth a pound of cure." And "Where there's a will, there's a way."

In the long versions, you have to spend so much time decoding the written symbols that the ideas themselves become obscured by the words.

That is not to say that you should never write a long sentence. But writers who habitually use long sentences become a nuisance to the reader because long sentences usually tangle ideas. Short sentences, on the other hand, add impact to the ideas they convey:

It is most important that this section be completed in its entirety because the executive research committee will be auditing our research plans in future quarters, and members are especially interested in how lab work done by employees in the E&P group relates to the plan of studies outlined for the three new chemists. Incomplete forms will be discarded.

You see how much more attention you give to the last sentence? That's because it's short.

In addition to length, the reader's pace through a document is also determined by the sentence pattern.

English sentences usually follow four basic patterns. The building blocks of these sentence patterns are clauses.

An *independent clause* has a subject and verb and stands alone:

The deliverability is increased by one-fifth.

A *dependent clause* has a subject and verb but does not express a complete thought. It must be attached to an independent clause for full meaning:

Because the deliverability is increased by one-fifth, . . .

The various sentence patterns are the simple, compound, complex, and compound-complex.

Simple sentences. Simple sentences contain only one independent clause. Simple sentences are usually direct and easy to read.

We estimated the radial position of the water front by planimetering the contact area.

Compound sentences. These sentences have two or more independent clauses. They divide the reader's attention and force consideration of two or more ideas at once. The reader, therefore, must slow his or her pace to concentrate on both.

> We estimated the radial position of the water front by planimetering the contact area; however, the accuracy of this determination depends on the model grid.

Complex sentences. These sentences have one independent clause and one or more dependent clauses. This structure adds peaks and valleys. Listen to the writer raise and lower her voice throughout the following example. The *although* clause is the beginning of the uphill climb. Gradually the reader trudges over the hill and then slides down to the main point in the last clause. Complex sentences add variety to writing and help emphasize the most important ideas.

> Although the slumping problem manifests itself most visibly in the enhanced gas recovery (EGR) predictions, it is also present in the primary depletion case.

Compound-complex sentences. The compound-complex sentence pattern has at least two independent clauses and at least one dependent clause. Compound-complex sentences really slow the reading pace. A reader has to follow the peaks and valleys while also concentrating on two equally important ideas. Most compound-complex sentences are too long for fast, easy comprehension.

> Because the optimal timing for ending water production will be very sensitive to aquifer description, the best opportunity will appear late in the project life; therefore, we should revise our timing estimate after we have evaluated aquifer response to water production.

In general, to get your point across clearly, quickly, and emphatically, prefer simple or complex sentences of 25 words or less.

6.2 Improper Subordination of Ideas

The way you link ideas in a sentence conveys both meaning and emphasis. Put the most important idea in the main clause and that clause in the most emphatic sentence position. Subordinate minor ideas.

Have you ever heard someone say, "I know what you said, but I don't know what you mean"? The implication is that the emphasis or interpretation of an idea is improper. Only you as the expert know how your ideas relate to each other and what key points need emphasis. You control the reader's interpretation by the way you link ideas.

To show you how powerful linking words and sentence positions can be, consider the difference in the messages of the following sentences:

> Tom pays his bills, but he's a real pain. (Maybe we shouldn't do business with him.)
>
> Tom's a real pain, but he pays his bills. (His business is worth the trouble.)
>
> Tom's a real pain, although he pays his bills. (An afterthought.)
>
> Although he's a real pain, Tom pays his bills. (Let's keep his business.)
>
> Tom pays his bills, and he's a real pain. (So? Reader is unsure of your point.)
>
> Tom's a real pain, and he pays his bills. (So? Reader is unsure of your point.)

Positioning your ideas for emphasis becomes more complicated the longer your sentence grows and the more linking words you add. Most simple sentences follow the subject-verb-object order. In such sentences, the subject gets the most emphasis, then the verb, and finally the object.

The most emphatic position in a complex sentence is at the end. The next most important position is the sentence beginning. The least important spot in a complex sentence is in the middle:

> Low-voltage heaters (80V) are used in cases where the heating elements will be attached to the vessel wall. (Emphasizes where the heating elements are attached.)
>
> In cases where the heating elements are attached to the vessel wall, low-voltage heaters (80V) are used. (Emphasizes the use of low-voltage heaters.)
>
> In cases where numerous branched cracks are present, the chance for complete removal of all cracks is diminished. (Emphasizes that the chance for removal is diminished.)
>
> The chance for complete removal of all cracks is diminished

in cases where numerous branched cracks are present. (Emphasizes the cases of numerous branched cracks.)

The reasons for our analysis, which we will detail on page 6, involve money and timing. (Emphasizes money and timing.)

The reasons for our analysis, which involve money and timing, are detailed on page 6. (Emphasizes the location of the details—page 6.)

Now let's put both ideas together—links and sentence positions. The following sentences illustrate proper and improper subordination.

Improper:

The crane barge will be put in position, and the old dolphin decking will be cut and removed from the jacket structure.

Proper:

With the crane barge in position, the old dolphin decking will be cut and removed from the jacket structure.

Improper:

CRA material is highly susceptible to mechanical damage, and operators must follow the correct handling procedure prior to any pipe or accessory movement.

Proper:

Because CRA material is highly susceptible to mechanical damage, operators must follow the correct handling procedure prior to any pipe or accessory movement.

Improper:

The summary is in the appendix and corrects earlier miscalculations by our investigators.

Proper:

The summary in the appendix corrects earlier miscalculations by our investigators.

Improper:

Put a magnetic penetrameter on the pipe OD. Apply the particle bath to the penetrameter head. The residual magnetic field strength must be strong enough to show a clear

---

The Purpose of Linking Words

Linking Words	Function
And, either/or, neither/nor	Link equal ideas
Therefore, so, because, thus, hence, consequently	Indicate a cause-and-effect relationship
When, as, then, while, next, later	Indicate time relationships
Because, although, while, where, if	Express subordinate ideas

---

Figure 6–1. The purpose of linking words. Linking words should convey the proper relationship between ideas.

indication on the penetrameter. It should be viewed under a blacklight. The indication must be oriented perpendicular to the direction of the field. Each joint must be checked with a penetrameter.

Proper:

With a magnetic penetrameter on the pipe OD, apply the particle bath to the penetrameter head. The residual magnetic field strength must be strong enough to show a clear indication on the penetrameter when viewed under a blacklight. The indication must be oriented perpendicular to the direction of the field. Each joint must be checked with a penetrameter.

Avoid linking your ideas randomly. Determine your most important idea and place it in the most emphatic part of the sentence. Link the minor ideas to that key idea with subordinating words to show the proper relationship, such as time, equality, or cause and effect (see as shown in **Figure 6–1**).

6.3   Non Sequiturs and Illogical Gaps

Each idea should logically build on the preceding ideas. The reader shouldn't be left with a "So what does that have to do with what you just said?" feeling.

Non sequitur is a Latin phrase meaning "It does not follow." Suppose you are watching a dramatic movie on TV. Your attention is totally absorbed by the action. Then the screen goes black and the sound is muffled with static. When the picture and dialogue resume, it's apparent you have missed something.

Readers often have the same frustrated feeling about ideas strung together without an apparent connection. In such cases, they are inclined to respond, "So what? I don't get your point." Consider the following examples.

> Margaret makes an enormous salary, **and** she drives an older model Ford. (So what's the point?)

> Margaret makes an enormous salary, **but** she drives an older model Ford. (Probably the point is that even though she could afford any model she wanted, she doesn't have much interest in prestigious cars.)

> John is divorcing Mary, **and** he took her to lunch. (So what's the point?)

> **Even though** John is divorcing Mary, he took her to lunch. (Probably the point is that they are still associating with each other.)

Such gaps in logic are much easier to detect in someone else's writing than in our own because writers are familiar with their subject matter. In any piece of technical writing, the ideas and the logic behind them probably seemed clear to the writer or he or she wouldn't have expressed them in such a way.

Consider the following:

> Corrosion pitting may be detected during the inspection. Pipe with excessive pitting and sharp gouges shall not be proved up with an ultrasonic thickness gauge and should be set aside.

Compare:

> Corrosion pitting may be detected during the inspection. **If** excessive pitting or sharp gouges are found, the pipe shall not be proved up with an ultrasonic thickness gauge. **Instead,** the damaged pipe should be set aside.

The following is very confusing:

> The testing equipment mentioned in the specifications costs

$10,480. A Bithurg Labs representative has proposed to re-evaluate the test results on our first samples. (So what's the point, the connection?)

But rewritten, the message is evident:

The testing equipment mentioned in the specifications costs $10,480; **therefore,** we may decide to wait before purchasing that new equipment. A Bithurg Labs representative has pro-posed to reevaluate the test results on our first samples **to determine if the equipment was the cause for the discrepancies.**

Make sure you leave no cracks between ideas for your reader to fall through and lose your line of reasoning.

6.4   Incomplete and Run-on Sentences

Every sentence must have a subject and verb and express a complete thought. As a general rule, keep one major idea to a sentence.

Fragments are careless errors usually created when writers glance over their words and see a subject and verb and assume they've finished the initial thought. A subject and verb alone do not a complete sentence make. If you remember from **Section 6.1,** a dependent clause has a subject and verb, but it does *not* express a complete thought.

Each of the following clauses has a subject and verb, but none expresses a complete thought without being linked to another idea: The lead-ins that often signal fragmentary thoughts are in bold print:

The fact that the 730 scans the entire page while loading only the windowed area into memory. (What about this fact?)

Interpretive or thematic maps, **which** use data like popula-tion, income, and sales statistics to analyze the characteristics of an area. (What about these maps? The *which* clause adds a subordinate idea, but the writer has not finished the main thought about interpretive or thematic maps.)

Because the extensive collection of library functions has been expanded for greater compatibility with UNEX System 2 and the TASI standard to provide a header file. (What is because?)

Although the magnetic field indicator is intended for use as an aid in determining the presence of magnetic fields and the direction of the lines of magnetic flux. (Although this, what?)

Deets Engineering, Inc., **being** solely oriented in the area of customer representation and customer services to provide quality control of oil and gas tubular goods and wellhead equipment. (What else about Deets Engineering, Inc.?)

First, **by reviewing** your individual safety programs utilized in your rig operations, and second, **by reviewing** your safety performance numbers submitted with each bid. (Then what? What happens by doing this reviewing?)

Just as confusing as incomplete sentences are those that run on and on and on and on—with too many ideas jammed together as if they constituted a single thought. "I am sick with a high fever I am going home" is a run-on sentence. Here are other examples:

Electromagnetic inspection (EMI) is the generic name for a common flaw-detection method used on OCTG products the principle of EMI is similar to magnetic particle inspection except that leakage fields near flaws are detected electronically instead of visually. (A period is required after *products*.)

The evaluation branch performs research and development to provide the USAF with advanced reliable and sensitive nondestructive inspection and evaluation techniques, and the NDE techniques satisfy pertinent inspection, evaluation, and quality assurance requirements and solve problems that arise in the production and in-service maintenance of USAF weapon systems, and sophisticated computer technology plays a key in such areas as signal processing, flaw characterizations and image construction/enhancement, inspection scanning control, and accept-reject decisionmaking. (This run-on sentence should be broken into three sentences.)

For single-phase problems that involve pure water, the natural choices for dependent variables are pressure and temperature, however, these variables are unsuitable for problems involving two-phase conditions where they become dependent on each other through the vapor-pressure curve. (A period is required after *temperature*. The thoughts on both sides of *however* are complete thoughts, and the sentence should be divided into two.)

Many writers get confused about run-on sentences that use connective adverbs such as *however, therefore, hence,* and *thus.* Commas are strong enough to separate two complete thoughts joined by *and, but, for, or, so,* or *yet.* But the longer connective adverbs cited above require a semicolon before them when the words on each side of the connective express a complete thought.

Incorrect:

> They have provided quantitative information on rates of natural recharge and discharge, however, Figure 4 shows temperature and pressure distribution calculated for a 2D vertical section. (A run-on sentence. Either add a semicolon before *however,* or insert a period and start a new sentence with *however.*)

Correct:

> Before adding the fluid, however, check the temperature. (*However* here is just an interrupter. The phrase preceding it does not make complete sense by itself.)

Either fragments mistaken as sentences or too many thoughts jammed together into one sentence make your writing unacceptable. Keep one major thought to a sentence—but make sure that thought is complete.

6.5 Parallel Structure

Structure sentences so that you express equal ideas in similar ways, using all verbs, all prepositional phrases, all adjectives, and so forth.

Actors and actresses often bicker over who gets top billing in a movie—who's the star and who's the co-star, who gets his or her name in two-inch letters and who must settle for half an inch.

Think of parallelism in this way. Two or more equal ideas in one sentence are fighting for the reader's attention, and you as the writer must treat them impartially. The equal ideas can be expressed with prepositional phrases, adverbial clauses, adjectives, or whatever; the forms of expression simply must match.

Consider the following examples of parallel and nonparallel structures.

Nonparallel:

> The technicians (1) **solved** the two-dimensional heat transfer problem by use of a finite element method, (2) have **identified** a set of three liquid crystal blends, (3) have **obtained** an estimate for *w* by direct measurement of the width, and (4) **developed** a method for combining the color mappings.

Parallel:

> The technicians (1) **solved** the two-dimensional heat transfer problem by use of a finite element method, (2) **identified** a set of three liquid crystal blends, (3) **obtained** an estimate for *w* by direct measurement of the width, and (4) **developed** a method for combining the color mappings. (Each item begins with the main verb.)

Nonparallel:

> The two major limitations of the method are **a limited sensitivity** and **that it is dependent on experimentally determining the width of the flaw directly from a liquid crystal color pattern.**

Parallel:

> The two major limitations of the method are **that its sensitivity is severely limited** and **that it is dependent on experimentally determining the width of the flaw directly from a liquid crystal color pattern.** (Two *that* clauses.)

Parallel:

> The two major limitations of the method are **its sensitivity** and **its dependency** on experimentally determining the width of the flaw directly from a liquid crystal color pattern. (Two noun phrases.)

Writing a nonparallel sentence is like wearing a brown shoe and a blue shoe to work.

6.6   Dangling Constructions

Descriptive words, phrases, and clauses tell more about another word or group of words in the sentence. The words that are modified must be on the page, not just in the writer's mind.

Almost any construction can become a dangler if the word or idea it modifies does not appear in the sentence. Some of the more common dangling constructions follow.

Dangler:

> After applying the appropriate pressure, the chart shows the
> various tools used. (The chart applied pressure?)

Correct:

> After applying the appropriate pressure, the technician stores
> the tools and charts the results.

Dangler:

> Determining if the indication is caused by a rejectable defect,
> the leakage field is investigated by the inspector. (The leak-
> age field determines?)

Correct:

> The inspector investigates the leakage field to determine if
> the indication is caused by a rejectable defect.

Dangler:

> Having identified the cause of the bleeding, the damaged
> spleen was removed by the surgeon. (The spleen identified
> the cause?)

Correct:

> Having identified the cause of the bleeding, the surgeon
> removed the damaged spleen.

Dangler:

> The sampling program has been questioned because of the
> random selections, thinking that the timing may have altered
> the pattern. (Who is thinking?)

Correct:

> The sampling program has been questioned because the
> timing may have altered the pattern of random selections.

Make sure descriptive words and phrases logically connect to
the rest of the sentence.

6.7   Commas That Change Meaning

Commas set off nonessential phrases and clauses from the rest of the sentence. Words and phrases that restrict or qualify the meaning of the words around them should not be set off with commas.

Commas can dictate meaning.

In the 1984 presidential election, the Republicans argued for two days over whether this statement from their platform should contain a comma: The Republicans oppose "any attempts to raise taxes which would harm the recovery."

In the previous statement, the door to raising taxes remained open. That is, the Republicans were opposed to raising harmful taxes, but they could decide to raise some taxes they thought would not harm the recovery.

Adding a comma to the sentence after *taxes* closed the door: The Republicans oppose "any attempts to raise taxes, which would harm the recovery." The latter statement means that any raise in taxes would harm the recovery.

If commas can play havoc in the hands of politicians, think what they can do in the hands of technical writers.

To conquer the most dangerous comma clarity problem, remember this general principle: Placing commas around a particular phrase or clause means that you can leave out the part set off by the commas and still keep the sentence meaning intact. Omitting commas around a particular phrase or clause means that those words are essential to the meaning of the entire sentence. Without commas to cut those words away, that essential phrase or clause qualifies or restricts the meaning of the rest of the sentence.

Consider the meaning of the following sentences with and without the commas.

Essential:

> The new deck that has already been fabricated and assembled includes the new mooring gear. (The *that* phrase specifies which deck.)

Nonessential:

> The new deck, which has already been fabricated and assembled, will be lifted and installed next month. (The *which* phrase adds nonessential information.)

Essential:

> There are 28 companies actively producing the injection-molded parts that we have considered using in our design. (The *that* clause tells which parts.)

Nonessential:

> There are 28 companies actively producing the injection-molded parts, which we have considered using in our design. (The *which* clause expresses an afterthought.)

Essential:

> The RMP maps have been redesigned to show the Hogan fields where we have already drilled. (Specific Hogan fields are indicated—the ones where we have drilled as opposed to the ones where we have not yet drilled.)

Nonessential:

> The RMP maps have been redesigned to show the Hogan fields, where we have already drilled. (The *where* clause expresses an afterthought, the idea that we have drilled in the Hogan fields.)

Essential:

> The three methods that are currently available for modeling the behavior of geothermal reservoirs are decline-curve analysis, the lumped-parameter method, and the distributed-parameter method. (The *that* clause is essential to the meaning. It specifies which three methods are available.)

Nonessential:

> The three methods, which are currently available for modeling the behavior of geothermal reservoirs, are decline-curve analysis, the lumped-parameter method and the distributed-parameter method. (The *which* clause provides additional information but does not distinguish these three methods from other methods.)

Commas carry clout; use them knowledgeably.

6.8   Misplaced Words, Phrases, and Clauses

Descriptive terms should be placed as close to the words they modify as possible.

The most frequently misplaced words in technical writing are the adverbs *almost, only, nearly, just,* and *even.* Such words inserted incorrectly can completely change sentence meaning. Compare the following sentences:

This berthing schedule will **only** permit construction activities to take place for 48 hours out of every 72-hour period. (The schedule will only permit the activities; that's all the schedule can do.)

This berthing schedule will permit construction activities to take place for **only** 48 hours out of every 72-hour period. (The schedule restricts construction to two-thirds of the time.)

Only this berthing schedule will permit construction activities to take place for 48 hours out of every 72-hour period. (Only this schedule, as opposed to other schedules, will permit construction activities as specified.)

The adverb *just* also has the power to alter your sentence meaning by limiting what follows it:

Just Joseph Holland has the authority to revise the specifications on the couplings. (No one else has the authority.)

Joseph Holland **just** has the authority to revise the specifications on the couplings. (He has authority only, not any ability or expertise in design.)

Joseph Holland has the authority **just** to revise the specifications on the couplings. (He has authority only to revise.)

Joseph Holland has authority to revise **just** the specifications on the couplings. (He can revise the specifications only—he cannot revise anything else, such as a brochure, pertaining to the couplings.)

Joseph Holland has authority to revise the specifications on **just** the couplings. (He cannot revise specifications on items other than the couplings.)

Almost can cause the same problems:

Almost all manufacturers' protectors were able to meet our test criteria in all these areas.

All manufacturers' protectors were **almost** able to meet our test criteria in all these areas.

All manufacturers' protectors were able to meet our test criteria in **almost** all these areas.

Misplaced *which* clauses also create havoc with sentence meaning:

The aluminum housings have been favorably compared with stainless steel inserts, **which experience abrasive wear at the entrances and exits.** (The inserts experience the wear.)

The aluminum housings, **which experience abrasive wear at the entrances and exits,** have been favorably compared with stainless steel inserts. (The aluminum housings experience the wear.)

The poron cellular urethane, **which must be specified in the client proposal,** warrants further consideration as the preferred product. (Poron cellular urethane must be specified in the proposal.)

The poron cellular urethane warrants further consideration as the preferred product, **which must be specified in the client proposal.** (Whatever product we prefer must be stated specifically.)

Isolate the specific word or phrase you intend to emphasize and then insert the descriptive terms immediately before or after that word or phrase.

6.9   Tense and Mood Changes

Report experimental work and results in the past tense. State facts, hypotheses, and general truths or conditions in the present tense. Don't change tenses or moods unnecessarily. To do so confuses your reader.

Verbs have tense and mood. That is, they show action or existence in either present, past, or future time. Mood reflects whether a statement is factual or conditional, gives a command, or states a strong wish or demand.

Indicative mood verbs state facts or ask questions:

Image scaling **permits** you to enlarge the saved image.

The system **prompts** you to format a disk.

Should all technical proposals **include** the May 1 deadline?

Imperative mood verbs give commands:

Format the disk before you install the program.

Reduce the pressure by 10 psi every half hour.

Show the data on a bar graph.

Subjunctive mood verbs express things not yet fact, such as conditions, concessions, strong wishes, or demands:

If they accept the proposal, we **would begin** construction August 2. (Condition)

Our engineers **would analyze** the samples if they had the proper testing apparatus. (Condition)

The ongoing experiment dictates that the daily data **be charted** immediately. (Demand)

We urge that the tanks **be monitored** for hydrogen leaks. (Strong wish)

Report experimental work and results in the past tense; use the present tense for hypotheses, facts, and general truths or ongoing conditions.

Past Work:

We **tested** the porosity of all products and **found** Bendine C to be the most suitable for our purposes. (Past tense)

General Truth:

The machinability of prealloyed iron powder with a higher Mn/S ratio **improves** when various mixes **compensate** for different strength levels. (Present tense)

Any time you change tenses unnecessarily, the reader becomes confused. Was your result a one-time occurrence or is it a general truth? Is the work completed or still underway? Is the outcome conditional or fact? Correct tense and mood choices prevent confusion. See **Figure 6–2** for examples of appropriate tense and mood changes.

Proper Use of Tense and Mood

The Chemstrip bG Test Strips **were tested** by the procedure listed on the container label. Results **were determined** by a comparison of the reacted and wiped strip to the color chart on the container label. The results **were selected** from a list of interpolation levels composed of the colorblock levels and three equally spaced levels in between the colorblock levels. The results of this study **are described** in three figures. Figure 12 **presents** a comparison of the two testing products. . . .

Figure 6–2. Proper use of tense and mood. The proper use of present and past tense in the same document separates existing conditions from experimental work and improves the clarity of a complicated report.

7

Precision
in Word and Phrase
Choices

7.1 Redundant Words and Phrases

Strip redundant words and phrases from your writing. Review your writing for such culprits as noun pairs expressing the same idea, verb add-ons, and other redundancies.

Redundancy in a document is much like stuttering in a speech—both detract from the ideas being presented. That is not to say that all repetition is bad; some writers repeat key phrases and ideas to serve as transitions between parts of a proposal or report and to reemphasize major points.

But redundancy is *needless* repetition, which has no place in effective writing.

Familiarize yourself with the following lists of common repetitious words and phrases (**Figures 7–1, 7–2,** and **7–3**) so that you can drop them from your own work. Additionally, pay attention to the "categories" of unnecessary repetition so you can recognize redundancy when using words and phrases specific to your own areas of expertise.

Paired Words Expressing the Same Idea

subject matter	facts and figures
goals and objectives	few in number
in this day and age	costs the sum of $222
period of time	during the month of August
point in time	during the years 1988–1998
brown in color	summer months
small in size	the reason is because
cylindrical in shape	the reason is why
a distance of 220 miles	first and foremost
the time of day	separate and distinct
200 words in length	ways and means

Figure 7–1. Paired words expressing the same idea. Use one or the other of each pair, but not both.

Verb Add-ons	
continue on	finish up
refer back to	open up
consolidated together	cancel out
grouped together	circulate around
joined together	first began
combined together	continue to remain
add together	still remain
add up	still continue
connect together	still persist
attach together	start out
try out	balance against each other

Figure 7–2. Verb add-ons. The verb alone is sufficient.

7.2   Precise Words and Phrases

Say what you mean—exactly. Repeating key words or phrases is preferable to using alternatives that distort what you intend to say.

The following paragraph (with names changed) is part of a memo from a client:

On page nine of Section I of your report, you commented that RWW has not charged the Venture for any amounts related to the "cost of money for facilities capital." John Duke of RWW has asked me to request that you clarify the meaning of the above-mentioned "cost of money for facilities capital" and additionally that you review the concept for the Far East operation.

Redundant Combinations

alternative choices	conclusive proof
desirable benefits	true facts
basic fundamentals	consensus of opinion
important essentials	final completion
basic essentials	advance warning
main essentials	adequate enough
serious crisis	disappear from sight
close together	following after
end result	equally as effective as
few and far between	any and all
final outcome	as a general rule
future plans	in actual fact
past experience	in two equal halves
past history	symptoms indicative of
early beginnings	completely surrounded
separate entities	on pages 20–30 inclusive
empty space	regular weekly meetings
close proximity	exactly alike
surrounding circumstances	precisely correct
joint partnership	

Figure 7–3. Redundant combinations. Redundancy indicates careless thinking and weakens the impact of your ideas.

When pointing out imprecise words to an engineer or geophysicist, frequently we hear the response, "But wouldn't it be clear in context?" No! The answer is almost always no. In the previous memo, why didn't the writer just say "interest on the real estate loan for the Tudor Lab" (or whatever) rather than the vague "cost of money for facilities capital"?

Don't Write:	You Could Be Specific:
major-incident response unit	ambulance, police car
technical exposures	error in the software
limited resources	limited staff, expertise, money
educational venture	seminar, correspondence course
several factors	cost, manpower, and safety
bad weather	hurricane
transportation systems	pipelines
storage facilities	warehouse, disk space
environmentally controlled	chemical-free
nurturing unit	parent

Some writers use less precise words as they move through their reports because of an idea from one of their English teachers who said, "Don't keep repeating the same word over and over—choose a synonym." The teacher admonished students to switch from *house* to *cottage* to *dwelling* to *residence.*

Let's give English teachers credit for helping students build a large vocabulary. But that's terrible advice for the technical writer. Once you have chosen the most precise word, stay with it. Repeating an effective, precise word is preferable to using a vague alternative. If, however, you can use alternative words without losing precision and creating confusion, by all means do so.

Additionally, to be precise means to understand both the denotation and the connotation of the words and phrases you choose.

Some words can be taken either positively or negatively—and will be, according to the experience and background of the reader. Consider this series of near synonyms: *surprising, interesting, novel, amusing,* and *revealing* (see **Figure 7–4** for others). Such word choices often leave translation open to readers, which is usually a dangerous thing to do.

To summarize: Simple, concrete words and phrases lead to effective writing.

Denotation and Connotation

Neutral	Positive	Negative
temporary	alternative	makeshift
strong	tenacious	obstinate
initial	pioneering	primitive
odorous	fragrant	foul smelling
inherent	essential	engrained
shelter	safeguard	conceal
change	stimulate	agitate
imitation	substitute	fake
altered	improved	replaced
firm	confident	opinionated
residence	home	hovel
satisfactory	ample	adequate
end	finish, conclude	abandon, terminate

Figure 7–4. Denotation and connotation. Be aware of unintended shades of meanings in the word you use.

7.3 Illogical Comparisons and Ideas

Think about the logic of words strung together and make sure they say what you mean.

Some technical writers struggle so long with a sentence that once they get the prepositional phrases and the adverbial clauses tucked into some out-of-the-way place, they fail to consider the logic of the sentence in its entirety.

To illustrate the common weakness of illogical comparisons and ideas, here are a few classics collected over the years:

I want to take a day out of your time to discuss this. (Not if I can help it! A day out of my schedule perhaps.)

The appreciation of a host-controlled environment will become not only the best way but the only way to implement
complexity of a distributed network. (Is the appreciation a
way? Why would they want to implement complexity—job
security?)

The question may no longer be valid for all brick walls—
changes in construction materials and methods jeopardize
its truthfulness. (How is it possible for a question to be true?
An answer can be, but not a question.)

A clear understanding of the conversion that will take place
is illustrated by the diagrams that follow. (The understanding
is illustrated? They have a diagram of brain waves?)

The following list of security coordinators has authority to
write policy statements. (The list is going to write the statements? Does that mean the coordinators themselves can go
home?)

Also illogical, although perhaps not obviously so to many writers,
are comparisons of adjectives such as *unique, extinct, fatal, matchless,
priceless*, and *permanent*. Something is either unique or it isn't. One
stab wound cannot be more fatal than another. Taxes are more permanent than death? Such comparisons show a basic misunderstanding of word meanings.

Finally, avoid incomplete or ambiguous comparisons.

Incomplete:

Our site readings varied more than your chemist.

Complete:

Our site readings varied more than those taken by your
chemist.

Incomplete:

The workflow in Diagram 6 is more complex than Diagram 7.

Complete:

The workflow in Diagram 6 is more complex than that shown
in Diagram 7.

To write clearly, you have to think clearly. Logic counts—in sentence construction as well as in research.

7.4 Jargon: When to Use It and When Not to Use It

When writing to professionals with technical backgrounds similar to yours, you may use the technical language of your field. When writing to a general audience, particularly decision makers with limited expertise in your technical field, avoid such jargon and select the simplest accurate words or phrases to express your ideas.

To really outstanding scientific writers and thinkers, jargon is out of place most of the time:

> Most of the fundamental ideas of science are essentially simple, and may, as a rule, be expressed in a language comprehensible to everyone.
> —Albert Einstein, *The Evolution of Physics*

> If you cannot—in the long run—tell everyone what you have been doing, your doing has been worthless.
> —Erwin Schrödinger, *Science and Humanism*

> Even for a physicist, the description, in plain language, will be a criterion of the degree of understanding that has been reached.
> —Werner Heisenberg, *Physics and Philosophy*

Although Webster's dictionary defines *jargon* as "the technical terminology or characteristic idiom of a specific activity or group," *jargon* has a negative connotation for most people. The term has come to mean obscure and often pretentious language used in an attempt to impress rather than to express.

We wouldn't dare to say that technical writers should or even could eliminate all the jargon from their writing. But we do think jargon should be used only sparingly in reports, proposals, and manuals intended for broad audiences with varying degrees of technical expertise.

Let clarity and consideration for your audience be your guides.

7.5   Misused Words and What the Spellchecker Can't Do

Awareness is the key to correcting misused words in your writing.

Mark Twain put it this way: "The difference between the right word and the almost-right word is the difference between lightning and the lightning bug." Never mind that Archie Bunker and Yogi Berra both became famous partly because of their malapropisms. Misused words hit readers like the proverbial bolt of lightning. Consider, for example, these sentences we recently discovered: "I will keep you posted on the action as it *accrues*" and "It was successful because of the limited marketing expense *occurred* in developing the revenue source."

The list of almost-right words is endless. We'll begin with a common misuse of *versus*. Writers often misuse *versus* or *vs.* to mean *and*, *or*, or *as compared to*. The correct meaning is *against* or *opposed to*. A paper entitled "In-house Sampling Programs versus External Sampling Programs" should be about *differences*, not similarities, in the two kinds of sampling programs.

Unfortunately, computer spellcheckers can't always help with such problems. They don't, for example, catch the misused *operative* for *operational*, *affect* for *effect*, or *insure* for *ensure*.

To rid your own writing of such mistakes, examine the list of commonly misused words given in **Figure 7–5** and make a mental note of them for your next writing project. Add to the list your own frequently misused words and verify each use in your writing.

Commonly Misused Words

Word	Definition
about	a guess or rough estimate, more or less
approximately	implies mathematical accuracy
accept	*verb*: to receive
except	*preposition*: not including

Figure 7–5. Commonly misused words. Misused words mislead your audience. Awareness is the key to deleting them from your writing.

Commonly Misused Words (continued)

Word	Definition
adapt	to adjust
adept	proficient
adopt	to choose
affect	*verb*: to influence or to involve
effect	*verb*: to cause; *noun*: a result
alternative	*noun*: another choice
alternate	*verb*: to repeat in a regular cycle
amount	applies to mass or bulk quantities
number	refers to separate units that can be counted
apt	suited, pertinent; inclined to; prompt to learn
liable	responsible for consequences
likely	probable
cite	*verb*: to give a reference, award, or traffic ticket
sight	*noun*: eyesight; *verb*: to see for the first time
site	*noun*: a location
continual	regular, but interrupted
continuous	constant and uninterrupted
data	plural when used to refer to facts or various pieces of information; singular when used to refer to a body of information

(continued on next page)

Figure 7–5 *(continued)*

Commonly Misused Words *(continued)*

Word	Definition
datum	archaic singular of *data*; a level surface or line used as a reference for measuring elevation
device	*noun*: a plan, procedure, technique, or object
devise	*verb*: to plan or to design
disinterested	impartial
uninterested	without interest in
farther	use for distance
further	use except for distance
fewer	use when quantity can be counted
less	use with quantity that cannot be counted
infer	listener or reader infers
implies	speaker or writer implies
material	*noun*: composition of something; *adjective*: pertinent
materiel	equipment, apparatus, supplies, inventory
may	indicates possibility
might	possibility, but indicates more uncertainty than *may*
operative	working
operational	ready to work
perspective	viewpoint
prospective	likely to become; expected

Figure 7–5 *(continued)*

Commonly Misused Words (continued)

Word	Definition
plain	*adjective*: simple, ordinary; *noun*: flat, treeless countryside
plane	*noun*: airplane, geometric surface, a tool; *verb*: to smooth or flatten
practical	useful or workable as opposed to theoretical
practicable	possible to practice or perform, feasible
precede	to go before
proceed	to move ahead
stationary	immobile
stationery	writing material

Figure 7–5 (continued)

7.6 Unnecessary Foreign Words and Phrases

The trend in both business and technical writing is to avoid foreign words and phrases. Use such words and phrases only if there is no good English equivalent.

Technical writing workshop participants frequently ask us to clarify the difference between *e.g.* and *i.e.* If so many technical professionals misunderstand the difference between the two, why use them? Why not write *for example* or *that is*?

Et cetera, meaning "and others of the same kind," is another frequently misused term.

Inappropriate:

In the meeting with the client you will need to bring your lab notebook, printouts of our analysis, etc.

What's the et cetera? A goat? Maybe a pail of water? This sentence establishes no clear pattern with which to identify what is to follow. Rather, the use of the term shows lazy thinking.

Appropriate:

> Table 6 clearly shows that the displacement values have increased in direct proportion to the addition of our Theyal mixture: 3 percent, 6 percent, 9 percent, 12 percent, etc. (A clear pattern is indicated.)

Our advice on foreign words and phrases is to use them only when there is absolutely no English equivalent!

Lists
Uses and Misuses

> *Lists are powerful attention getters. They catch the eye of skimming readers, making it easy to overview and review key ideas. Therefore, use lists to highlight important points. Bulleted lists convey the idea that the listings are not exhaustive. Enumerated lists usually indicate some order, such as a chronological sequence of actions. List items in parallel form and punctuate in one of three ways: as phrases, as individual sentences, or as one sentence with a lead-in.*

Lists draw immediate attention to the ideas they present. Did you skim through this book before buying it? If so, your eyes probably were immediately directed to the lists on the pages you skimmed. The list format is like a red flag saying, "This is important, reader."

Therefore, use lists to do the following:

- Highlight major ideas in your reports, proposals, manuals, or correspondence
- Break down complex information into smaller, more manageable chunks
- Overview key information quickly
- Review key information quickly

On the other hand, the misuse of a list for unimportant information confuses readers. If they find minutiae too often in a list format, readers become distrustful of all your lists.

Overuse is another abuse of the list format. Any technique for emphasizing—whether boldfacing, underlining, or italicizing—loses its effectiveness if overused.

Bullets or Numbers?

To set off items in a list, use either bullets or numbers. Bulleted lists indicate items that do not necessarily constitute an exhaustive listing or are perhaps separate ideas altogether. Enumerated lists most often convey a chronological sequence, such as a sequence of actions.

Parallel Structure

For faster reading and skimming, make sure that each item in a list is in parallel form. That is, all items should be either sentences, phrases, or words. Also, items should begin alike—either all verbs, all adjectives, all nouns, and so forth. Lists can be in any one of several formats, as shown in **Figure 8–1.**

Three Ways to Punctuate a Formal List

<u>No End Punctuation on Separate Items</u>

Therefore, use lists for:

- highlighting major ideas in your reports, proposals, manuals, or correspondence
- breaking down complex information into smaller, more manageable chunks
- overviewing key information quickly
- reviewing key information quickly

<u>End Punctuation on Complete Sentences</u>

Why use lists?

- Major ideas can be highlighted in your reports, proposals, manuals, or correspondence.
- Complex paragraphs can be broken down into smaller, more manageable chunks.
- Key information can be quickly overviewed.
- Key information can be quickly reviewed.

<u>Punctuation as One Long Sentence</u>

Use lists to present

- major ideas in your reports, proposals, manuals, or correspondence,
- complex information in smaller, more manageable chunks,
- key information for quick overview,
- key information for quick review.

Figure 8–1. Three ways to punctuate a formal list. Items in a list should be in parallel form, but there can be variety in format and punctuation.

How to Punctuate
Formal and Informal Lists

When punctuating a formal list, you have three choices: (1) no end punctuation on the separate items, (2) end punctuation for all items that are complete sentences, and (3) punctuation that makes the list lead-in and all separate items into one long sentence. You do not have the option, however, to skip from one format to another in the same list. The first sentence in this paragraph is an example of an informal list—one not set off with indentation or bullets. See **Figure 8–1** for examples of how to punctuate a formal list.

9

Analogies
When to Use Them
and How to Develop Them

Analogies make technical concepts clear and memorable. They can also replace entire paragraphs of less-effective description. To develop good analogies, always base them on concepts, functions, objects, or behaviors familiar to the reader.

A decade ago, many sales representatives explained word processors to customers this way: "Basically, this directory on the screen is like your filing cabinet. You see all the files listed here. When you highlight the file you want and press ENTER, it's like having the file open on your desk. You can now move words around and enter things into the document, just as you would do with an open paper file." The analogy was a good one. Customers got the picture and quickly learned how word processors work.

To record management experts, the statistician presents storage problems this way: "We create enough paperwork in the corporate world each year to paper the globe four times."

To biology students, the professor explains, "The eye operates much like a camera. The retina is the film. . . ."

An analogy provides one of the best tools available for technical writers to convey major ideas with an impact. A chemist recently showed us an excellent report he had completed on his research and on the development of a new product. After presenting the long chemical equations, he had summarized in this way: "The consistency of this product will be much like shaving cream."

He effectively expressed with one analogy what would have taken a paragraph of detailed description to convey.

Good analogies either establish or extend a reader's understanding of objects, functions, relationships, or behaviors. Some analogies can be short, as short as one sentence. Other analogies (such as the analogy between a camera and the human eye) may require three or four paragraphs in order to present all the similarities in appearance, function, and performance.

Remember that an analogy *clarifies* an idea and makes it easy to remember, but an analogy *never proves* anything. Writers should never point out similarities and then conclude that because two things are alike in a few ways, they are alike in all ways. Analogies amplify, clarify, and specify, but they never justify (see **Figure 9–1**).

So how do you develop good analogies? The key is finding a basis of comparison familiar to your reader. If both of the concepts in the analogy are unfamiliar to the reader, all effect is lost.

Technical Analogies

The human eye is nature's best camera. The iris and the pupil act as the lens and shutter of the camera in that they control the depth of focus. The smaller the hole the photographer looks through, the greater the depth of focus and the sharper the picture. And like the modern camera's automatic lens adjustor, the pupil of the eye also gets smaller or larger according to available light. Likewise, when we squint or turn our head toward or away from bright light, or add sunglasses, we duplicate the photographer's manual adjustment of the camera's shutter speed to allow more or less light inside the camera.

Another similarity is that both the crystalline lens of the eye and the camera lens regulate where and how the image will focus on the retina of the eye or on the film. This image is inverted on the retina or film. The optic nerve sends the picture to the human brain for conversion to the picture we see; in film processing, the negative image is also reversed in the final photo. Finally, just like the camera's lens holder, the zonule of zinn, which is part of the ciliary body, holds the lens and its aperture in place during even the most strenuous movement.

● ● ●

The flow of charged particles (electrical current) through a conductor is like the flow of river water. In both cases, the current is simply the movement of matter through the medium. Matter can occupy space within the channel boundaries (electrons in the conductor, water in the river), but not until the matter is acted upon by an outside force will current flow. In the case of the river, this outside force is gravity, which creates a difference in potential energy between the high end and the low end of the river. For the conductor, this outside force is voltage, the difference in electrical potential energy between the two ends of the conductor. Finally, the electrical resistance of the conductor can be pictured as clogging debris in the river channel. High resistance in the conductor will impede electrical current just as a clogged and tortuous river channel will reduce the rate of water flow.

Figure 9–1. Technical analogies. Analogies improve clarity and make ideas memorable.

It is also important to consider how extensive the analogy is. In other words, are the two objects, functions, or processes alike in only one way or several? The more similar points, the better.

Technical writers who do not use analogies are overlooking a powerful tool for making their concepts clear and memorable.

10

Emphasis

10.1   General Layout of a Document

The framework of every document should be apparent to the reader. Either explain the layout or make it obvious by using informative headings and adequate white space to highlight prominent ideas and guide readers from major division to major division. The positions of most emphasis are the beginning of a document and the beginning of each section.

When walking into a house for the first time, most people glance around to get the "lay of the land." Their eyes look straight ahead and then dart to the left and right—to the family room, the formal living and dining areas, perhaps the kitchen. Then their eyes follow the hallway to the bedrooms and the game room upstairs.

Checking into a hotel, guests do the same thing: On the way to their room, they note the locations of the dining areas, vending machines, pool, exercise rooms, and fire exits.

Readers generally react the same way when examining a document for the first time; they glance at the table of contents and then thumb through the pages to see what they will find where. When they see fields of unbroken prose, they know reading the document is going to be like a trip to the dentist: It may be good for them, but they'll hate it. Therefore, writers must do everything possible to help readers find their way around; the methods for doing this are many and varied.

For example, you may guide the reader's attention by the relative space devoted to various details and ideas, the omission of details, the position and order of ideas, listings, visuals, repetition, word choice, and typographical effects.

The framework of a document is to a reader what a road map is to a traveler.

10.2   The Beginning:
The Most Prominent Position

Satisfy the curiosity of your primary readers first: Give their information a prominent position in your document. Secondary readers may need to look further into a document for the details of interest to them.

Just as the home entryway and the hotel lobby get the visitor's primary attention upon arrival, the beginning or "entryway" of a document is the most prominent spot.

Therefore, writers of long documents should provide an executive summary up front so that readers can get an overview of the document first.

In a proposal, the benefits of what is being proposed should precede the specifications because buyers are most interested in what your product or service can do for them.

In a manual, how to operate equipment or perform a task goes up front in the most prominent position because that's of primary interest to the manual user.

Effective writers know better than to waste the reader's attention on introductions containing superfluous information or other "warmup drills" before getting to the most important points of a document.

The same principle of prominence holds true throughout each section of a document. Effective documents have a series of "mini" overview statements, followed by elaboration in later paragraphs.

You can also make your ideas easily accessible to the reader by providing frequent informative headings. Headings such as "Scope," "Discussion," "Procedures," "Results," "Conclusions," and "Recommendations" are so standard they give readers only the most general ideas as to what they'll find within the sections. If you still insist on generic headings such as these, be sure to provide informative subheads under each.

As an example of dynamic headings, consider these used by editor John C. Bittence to present his key points in highlighted form:

Al-Li Alloys—Watch for Porosity
Intermetallics—Heat Treatment Helps
Metal-Matrix Composites—CDW Works
Superalloys—Watch the Boron
Stainless—New Thoughts on Duplex
Titanium—Basically User Friendly
Rapidly Solidified Alloys—Weld with Care[1]

For a good test of whether you have effective headings, skim just the headings rather than the text. If you can't tell what the report says from the headings, they aren't effective. Contrast headings and overview statements in **Figures 10–1** and **10–2** to see how a document framework emphasizes key points.

---

[1]John C. Bittence, "Welding the Advanced Alloys," *Advanced Materials and Processes Inc. Metal Progress*, December 1987, pp. 35–39. Reprinted by permission of publisher.

Alternatives

The alternatives to this project are as follows:

A.   Graham could install a smaller-diameter pipeline, thereby reducing the capital cost, albeit a small reduction. The material cost of the proposed 20″ pipe, valves, and fittings is $1.64 million; therefore, any reduction in diameter will have minimal impact on the overall project cost of $9.06 million. Also, the smaller-diameter line would not be adequate to provide additional transportation and sales services. Future pipeline looping (necessary to provide additional gas service) cannot be performed along the existing pipeline route due to the area's population density and limited right-of-way width. Therefore, should Graham wish to provide additional future gas services, a new pipeline would have to be constructed *around* Baton Rouge. This new pipeline would increase the distance, thereby greatly increasing the pipeline's cost.

B.   Graham could derate the existing pipeline (i.e., reduce the pipeline's operating pressure), thereby reducing the potential for future failures due to corrosion within the deteriorated pipe joints. However, the pressure reduction *will not* lessen the likelihood of future failures of the Franklin couplings, a consideration of paramount importance from a safety standpoint.

C.   Graham could abandon the pipeline in place. Abandonment would require Graham to apply for a FERC abandonment certificate and possibly to renegotiate existing sales and transportation/exchange agreements (necessary to modify the term). An abandonment order would likely be granted only if FERC has evidence that Graham's existing customers along Phase II can be provided comparable service—volumes and prices—by some other gas supplier. Once they take the pipeline out of service, Graham would lose revenues from existing and potential transportation and sales transactions.

D.   The risk of failure of Franklin couplings due to the adverse impact of nearby construction can be reduced by the use of weld-over sleeves. An average of 20 weld-over sleeves, costing $1,000 each, are installed each year on this pipeline segment. However, a sleeved Franklin coupling is not the structural equivalent of a welded pipe joint, and there will be no gains in maintenance-cost savings or operating flexi-

Figure 10–1. Intimidating layout. Overview statements and key ideas are buried in a crowded, intimidating layout.

bility. Furthermore, routine "pigging" of the pipeline to remove impurities or water that enter the line from gas wells will be time consuming and very difficult. Finally, the sheer magnitude of the number of couplings to be sleeved, approximately 3000 for Phase II alone, makes this an impractical option. Reinforcing all the Franklin couplings with weld-over sleeves would cost over $4 million, including materials, labor, right-of-way, and damages. Additionally, the MAOP would remain at 300–500 PSIG per DOT requirements, which gives sales and transport no opportunity to increase volumes. Even with this "fix," the line pipe would still be very old. Any increase in pressure would be hazardous, again because of the Franklin couplings and the age of the line. Additionally, in order to reinforce all Franklin couplings, most of the line must be exposed to ensure that every coupling has been located. Because these couplings are installed so close to each other (10–20 feet), this work would require an expense similar to that needed for the proposed total replacement project. For all these reasons, the installation of the weld-over sleeves is not a sound alternative. It entails a large investment but does not solve the problem.

None of these alternatives were deemed to be viable because either they did not ensure safe and reliable service or they did not provide any capacity for future revenue-generating possibilities.

Figure 10–1. *(continued)*

Overview Statements and Easy-to-Skim Layout

Committee Findings on the Graham Pipeline Upgrade

Rejected Alternatives

major overview { The committee has studied the following alternatives and has determined them to be unsatisfactory. Either the alternatives were not sufficient to ensure safe and reliable service or they did not provide any capacity for future potential revenue-generating possibilities. Each requires a large investment without solving the problem.

Figure 10–2. Overview statements and easy-to-skim layout. Prominent overview statements with informative headings and uncrowded layout improve clarity.

overview of section

A. Install Smaller-Diameter Pipeline

Installing a smaller-diameter pipeline will not solve the existing problem and will be prohibitively expensive over the long term.

Only the initial capital cost for a smaller-diameter pipeline would amount to a small price reduction. The material cost of the proposed 20″ pipe, valves, and fittings is $1.64 million; therefore, any reduction in diameter will have minimal impact on the overall project cost of $9.06 million.

Also, the smaller-diameter line would not be adequate to provide additional transportation and sales services. Future pipeline looping (necessary to provide additional gas service) cannot be performed along the existing pipeline route due to the area's population density and limited right-of-way width. Therefore, should Graham wish to provide additional future gas services, a new pipeline would have to be constructed *around* Baton Rouge, which would increase the distance and thereby greatly increase the pipeline's cost.

overview of section

B. Derate Existing Pipeline

Graham could derate the existing pipeline (i.e., reduce the pipeline's operating pressure), thereby reducing the potential for future failures due to corrosion within the deteriorated pipe joints. However, the pressure reduction will not lessen the likelihood of future failures of the Franklin couplings, a consideration of paramount importance from a safety standpoint.

overview of section

C. Abandon the Pipeline in Place

Once Graham takes the pipeline out of service, we will lose revenues from existing and potential transportation and sales transactions.

Additionally, abandonment would require Graham to apply for a FERC abandonment certificate and possibly to renegotiate existing sales and transportation/exchange agreements. An abandonment order would likely be granted only if FERC has evidence that Graham's existing customers along Phase II can be provided comparable service by some other gas supplier.

Figure 10–2. *(continued)*

91

Overview Statements and Easy-to-Skim Layout
(continued)

D. Install Weld-Over Sleeves

overview of section { Sleeving all Franklin couplings on the line is not a reasonable method of ensuring the long-term safe operating integrity of the line.

Granted, the risk of failure of Franklin couplings due to the adverse impact of nearby construction can be reduced by the use of weld-over sleeves. (An average of 20 weld-over sleeves costing $1,000 each are installed each year on this pipeline segment.)

However, a sleeved Franklin coupling is not the structural equivalent of a welded pipe joint, and there will be no maintenance savings or gain in operating flexibility.

Furthermore, with couplings, routine "pigging" of the pipeline to remove impurities or water that enter the line from gas wells will be time consuming and very difficult.

Finally, the sheer magnitude of the number of couplings to be sleeved, approximately 3000 for Phase II alone, makes this an impractical option. Reinforcing all the Franklin couplings with weld-over sleeves would cost over $4 million, including materials, labor, right-of-way, and damages. Additionally, the MAOP would remain at 300–500 PSIG per DOT requirements, which gives sales and transport no opportunity to increase volumes. Even with this "fix," the line pipe is still very old. Any increase in pressure would be hazardous, again because of the Franklin couplings and the age of the line.

In order to reinforce all Franklin couplings, most of the line must be exposed to ensure that every coupling has been located. Because these couplings are installed so close to each other (10–20 feet), this work would require an expense similar to that needed for the proposed total replacement project.

Figure 10–2. *(continued)*

One last caution: Be careful about placing a stray fact under an inappropriate heading in an inappropriate section of your document. Pity the poor reader who, like Diogenes, will forever search unrewarded for the one thing he seeks.

10.3   Position of Ideas Within a Paragraph

The most prominent position in a paragraph is the first sentence. To emphasize key points, place them at the beginning of paragraphs instead of burying them in the middle or at the end.

Some technical writers are surprised to learn that not all readers on their distribution lists read all the details included in their reports or proposals. Readers like to skim where they can. Therefore, writers need to make sure readers pick up key points by placing them prominently in each section.

To illustrate how much placement of key ideas has to do with comprehension, read the following paragraph and determine the main idea:

> Much of the gain in the use of oil and gas has been for transportation, household, and commercial uses, for which coal is considerably less suitable. However, 27 percent of the oil and about 64 percent of the natural gas are used for industrial and electric utility purposes, many of which, from an efficiency standpoint, could be served equally well by coal. Oil and gas are preferred for convenience and cleanliness and, especially in the case of natural gas, for economic reasons. But coal has other serious problems in competing for today's energy market—the emission of particulate matter and sulfur dioxide. Technology is available for the control of particulates by electrostatic precipitators. However, despite numerous advertisements and claims to the contrary, no full-size, commercial-scale process for the removal of sulfur from stack gases has been operated successfully and continuously in the United States for a long enough time to be considered fully proved. Some are reported to do the job when operating, but operations have been intermittent because of technical difficulties. Some foreign processes are reported to be successful, but questions remain as to whether their performance can meet U.S. conditions and requirements.

When we ask workshop participants to summarize the main point, we get answers such as the following:

- Oil and gas are preferred for convenience, cleanliness, and economic reasons.

- Oil and gas are preferred for household use.
- Coal is less efficient for fuel use than either oil or natural gas.
- Requirements for fuel usage are too stringent in the United States.

The same kind of confusion results when a writer fails to summarize the key point in the first sentence of a paragraph.

Notice that when we revise the earlier example and place the overview statement in the most prominent position, the main idea gets most attention and all the other details become clearer.

> **Coal has serious problems competing in today's energy market.** Much of the gain in the use of oil and gas has been for transportation, household, and commercial uses, for which coal is considerably less suitable. However, 27 percent of the oil and about 64 percent of the natural gas are used for industrial and electric utility purposes, many of which, from an efficiency standpoint, could be served equally well by coal. Oil and gas are preferred for convenience and cleanliness and, especially in the case of natural gas, for economic reasons.
>
> **However, the most serious problem that coal has in competing is the emission of particulate matter and sulfur dioxide.** Technology is available for the control of particulates by electrostatic precipitators. Unfortunately, despite numerous advertisements and claims to the contrary, no full-size, commercial-scale process for the removal of sulfur from stack gases has been operated successfully and continuously in the United States for a long enough time to be considered fully proved. Some are reported to do the job when operating, but operations have been intermittent because of technical difficulties. Some foreign processes are reported to be successful, but questions remain as to whether their performance can meet U.S. conditions and requirements.

Only you, the writer, know what you want to emphasize. You signal the reader about your key point by placing it in the most prominent paragraph position—the beginning sentence.

10.4   The Climactic Sentence

In a simple sentence, the most prominent positions are those of the subject, the verb, and then the object. When

complex sentences present two ideas, the most impor-
tant idea should be in the main clause at the end of the
sentence.

John kicks the ball. Mary kicks the ball. See John and Mary kick the ball.

Such are the basics of our English sentence—subject, verb, object. The subject (John, Mary) gets the most attention; when we want to know more about the subject, we read the verb.

Study the following sentences illustrating lackluster writing. Note that in the weak examples the least important idea inappropriately serves as the sentence subject.

Weak:

> **It appears** that only a small amount of the product is available in the reactor effluent.

Emphatic:

> **Only a small amount of the product** is available in the reactor effluent. (Emphasizes the small amount.)

Weak:

> **There was** a load of 1,950 pounds per support that was used in our analysis.

Emphatic:

> **A load of 1,950 pounds per support** was used in our analysis. (Emphasizes the weight.)

Weak:

> **It has been suggested** that the product be evaluated as a defogging component.

Emphatic:

> **That the product be evaluated as a defogging component** has been suggested. (Emphasizes the product as a possible defogging component.)

When dealing with *two ideas* in a sentence, the most emphatic position is at the end of the sentence. In other words, climactic sentences (also called periodic sentences) create suspense by building to a climax.

Nonclimactic:

> The surface over which the inspection head must pass should be clean and free of scale, rust, dirt, oil, grease, or loose paint to ensure accurate test results. (Emphasizes the reason.)

Climactic:

> To ensure accurate test results, the surface over which the inspection head must pass should be clean and free of scale, rust, dirt, oil, grease, or loose paint. (Emphasizes the clean surface.)

Nonclimactic:

> We have postponed the testing because the client still has economic and environmental safety concerns.

Climactic:

> Because the client still has economic and environmental safety concerns, we have postponed the testing. (Emphasizes the postponement.)

Nonclimactic:

> We evaluated the corresponding isopropyl esters after we experienced problems with the acids.

Climactic:

> After we experienced problems with the acids, we evaluated the corresponding isopropyl esters. (Emphasizes what they did—the evaluation.)

This is not to say that *all* your sentences should be emphatic or climactic. Only you know which ideas you want to emphasize, and the placement of those ideas signals your reader about their importance. Sometimes you want to slow your readers down, sustaining interest over several ideas instead of leading them quickly through peaks and valleys. Simply be aware of the climactic technique for emphasizing key points.

10.5 Proportion

The amount of space devoted to the discussion of a particular idea suggests the importance of that idea.

When telling a good story, the entertainer carefully sets the stage, creates the mood, fills in the details, and then finally gets to the punch line. The bulk of the words create the situation; only the punch line brings the laugh.

Technical writers must use a different approach to present their stories. They must be careful not to get carried away with what's of interest only to them—perhaps the procedure or the testing. Technical professionals tend to write more about what they know the best, what interests them personally, and what took them the longest time to discover and interpret. Those details may not be the most important to other readers. In particular, the decision maker's interest will lie primarily in the punch line—the outcome, the conclusions, and the recommendations.

Effective writers, therefore, let the reader's interest dictate how much detail is required in each section of a document.

A situation occasionally arises, however, when the writer has to give certain details before the reader can grasp the most important idea, the conclusion. When that's the case, writers must use one of two techniques to keep the reader interested:

- Make the document layout apparent so that a reader can easily skip any unwanted details and get to the key point.
- Continue to remind the reader throughout the sections containing the details that the main point is coming.

Generally, there is no disharmony between bulk of words and emphasis; you can easily devote the most words and space to the most important ideas. Selection is the key.

10.6 Repetition

Repetition can be effective for emphasizing ideas within a paragraph or from section to section of a document. But each repetition of an idea should add something to the original thought.

Because of the pyramid structure of news stories, journalists become masters of repetition. The first paragraph of a news story gives the reader the nutshell version. Then as readers proceed through the remainder of the story, they find more elaboration on each of the first paragraph ideas. A new quote, a new fact, a new interpretation—all add to the original overview statement of the news item.

Likewise, repetition can be effectively used to help readers grasp and remember complex points in technical writing. But each restatement of an idea must add something—a new viewpoint, a more authoritative wording, a more specific or a broader application.

Study the uses of repetition in the following passage to understand its effectiveness in emphasizing and reminding the reader of the key issues under discussion (boldface added).

> **Our conclusion that nocturnal hypoglycemia does not cause clinically important fasting hyperglycemia in patients with IDDM is supported by the data of Periello and coworkers.** Using a somewhat different study design, they found that fasting plasma glucose concentrations averaged 129 mg per deciliter (7.1 mmol per liter) after nocturnal hypoglycemia and 112 mg per deciliter (6.2 mg per deciliter) after prevention of hypoglycemia in six patients with IDDM; plasma glucose values measured after blood sampling alone were not reported.
>
> When fasting hyperglycemia occurs in a patient with IDDM, a physician commonly considers two diametrically opposed actions. One assumes either that the fasting hyperglycemia is the result of too little insulin and alters the insulin regimen to increase insulin action in the hours before breakfast, or assumes that the hyperglycemia is the result of antecedent hypoglycemia (the Somogyi phenomenon) and alters the regimen to decrease insulin action earlier in the night. **The present findings do not support the latter approach. Indeed, we submit that current clinical and experimental data, as well as our present report, do not support the inclusion of nocturnal hypoglycemia in the differential diagnosis of fasting hyperglycemia in patients with IDDM.**[2]

Repetition has the same effect in writing as it does in an oral debate when debaters make their key points and then repeat them in as many ways as possible.

10.7   Special Effects: Informative Headings, Listings, Graphics, Typographical Effects, White Space, Color

Be creative in using special effects to direct your reader's attention to important ideas. Such special effects include

---

[2]Excerpted from material originally appearing in Karen M. Tordjman, M.D., et al., "Nocturnal Hypoglycemia in Patients with IDDM," *New England Journal of Medicine* 317 (1987): 1556. Reprinted by permission of publisher.

informative headings, listings, graphics, typographical effects, white space, color.

All words and paragraphs should not be created equal. Pages and pages of information presented in routine paragraph after routine paragraph can hold the attention of only the most ardent reader. Other readers need help in sorting major ideas from minor ideas.

Writers can help direct attention to important ideas by any number of special effects: informative headings; listings; italics, bold-face, or underlining; graphics; unusual typefaces, spacing, or line height; white space; color; one-sentence paragraphs; short, pithy statements.

Of course all of these devices can be overdone so that they become distracting. But that's a danger few technical writers need worry about.

The point can best be illustrated with the "before" and "after" versions in **Figure 10–3**.

Use of Special Effects

Version 1

Proposed Repair Plan

TRX proposes the following plan to finish repairing all of the Type 4 sites on the Belco-Gilmer pipeline system. This plan will ensure that, at a minimum, 60 percent of the pipe wall is remaining.

- Replace 9 sections (620 feet) of pipe on the Dolphin section where Type 4 internal corrosion exists. This work could be completed in the second quarter of 19—.

- Add one block valve on either side of the Little Williams Creek bottom. This section of the pipeline has the lowest elevation in the entire system (150 feet compared to the maximum 450). This work could be completed in the third quarter of 19—.

- Install scraper traps at Mt. Montgomery and Grayson stations. This installation will allow for monthly scrapers to be run in the remaining sections of the system. This section should have fewer corrosion problems than any other section. This work could be completed in the fourth quarter of 19—.

(continued on next page)

Figure 10–3.   Use of special effects. Special effects such as inform-ative headings, boldface, italics, underlining, and adequate white space guide the reader to key points.

Use of Special Effects *(continued)*

Version 2

Proposed Repair Plan

TRX proposes the following plan to finish repairing all of the Type 4 sites on the Belco-Gilmer pipeline system. This plan will ensure that, at a minimum, **60 percent of the pipe wall is remaining.**

- Dolphin Section: Replace 9 sections (620 feet) of pipe on the Dolphin section where Type 4 internal corrosion exists.

  Proposed completion: **Second quarter**

- Little Williams Creek Bottom: Add one block valve on either side of the Little Williams Creek bottom. This section of the pipeline has the lowest elevation of the entire system (150 feet compared to the maximum 450).

  Proposed completion: **Third quarter**

- Mt. Montgomery and Grayson Stations: Install scraper traps at Mt. Montgomery and Grayson stations. This installation will allow for monthly scrapers to be run in the remaining sections of the system. This section should have **fewer corrosion problems** than any other section.

  Proposed completion: **Fourth quarter**

Figure 10–3 *(continued).*

11

Persuasion

11.1   What Is a Persuasive Structure?

Technical writing must be persuasive—either to moti-
vate others to accept an idea, to abandon an idea, to take
action, or to spend money. A persuasive structure for a
technical report or proposal is one in which the writer
controls the flow and interpretation of ideas.

"We just give the facts," a chemist commented in front of his boss. "Management makes the decisions."

He was only partially right. Someone else may make decisions based on a technical writer's conclusions, but the writing must still be persuasive. In fact, even the most renowned scientists publish their important facts, discoveries, and conclusions in their respective professional journals and wait to see if their presentations of the "facts" withstand the scrutiny of their peers. Did they make errors in sampling? Did they introduce some bias into the process? Were their explanations of the findings the most plausible?

Facts are only the foundation of a technical report. True, the facts must be solid or the structure will crumble. But usually the inferences that the writer draws from the facts (conclusions) and the logical course of action he or she outlines (recommendations) will be far more useful to a reader than bald facts.

To put it succinctly, management needs advice from its technical staff. Therefore, technical writers must be persuasive. Should the company continue to fund research on a pet project that seems stymied? Should the organization propose a new project that has possibilities? Which research projects should management approve and continue if some of them must be eliminated from the budget? Is a new product or service marketable? How is it different from what's on the market already? All such questions call for persuasive writing.

Scientific writers, in fact, can never be completely objective. They must outline the plan of study and the sampling and testing procedures. They must decide which facts to present and which to omit. They must judge whether sampling errors were "small" or "significant." They must choose among neutral, positive, and negative synonyms to convey their findings: "malodorous," "intolerable," "promising."

When technical specialists say they don't need to be persuasive, that's a good indication that they have a misconception of their calling or that their writing needs improvement.

So why isn't persuasive writing simply a matter of presenting the facts and letting the facts speak for themselves? Examine this paragraph of uninterpreted facts:

> If Hilco takes gas into the system at the TG#1 location rather than at TG#2, Hilco will have to obtain the right-of-way and install about 15,000 feet of 6" pipe plus regulator and odorizer. The city is expanding toward the northeast in the direction of the proposed construction, and this expansion would make this right-of-way acquisition expensive and difficult to obtain. However, we could probably get permission from Roggett, Inc., to work in their right-of-way and purchase only a minimum width from other property owners. I think we would need a minimum of six months to gain this right-of-way for the TG#1 location.

So does the writer want us to take gas into the system at the TG#1 or the TG#2 location? Who knows? This wishy-washy presentation of facts needs a shaping hand to be persuasive.

If you've ever served as a juror, you will know the danger of an uncontrolled flow of "facts." The 12 jurors hear the same witnesses, examine the same evidence, digest the same summations by the lawyers, and remember the same instructions from the judge. Then they go to the jury room; 6 vote not guilty and 6 want to "hang 'em high."

Why with the same set of facts do people come to different conclusions? The issue is interpretation and control. Witness Harper tells her story. Juror Jones believes Harper's accounting of the events; Juror Smith does not. Facts and the intrepretation of facts are clearly different matters.

They come together, however, when you as a writer control your information and can present it persuasively. Unfortunately, which arrangement is most persuasive will depend on the reader's bias.

If you're writing to outsider readers who may be totally uninterested in what you have to say, put your conclusion and then the strongest evidence or reasons up front to get attention. If readers stop reading early, they still will have learned your main points.

If you're writing to internal readers who are presumably interested and have a stake in what you have to say, you may assume they will give you a fair hearing and read your entire report. Even so, always use a descending order.

If, on the other hand, you know your readers will be deadset against what you propose, begin with a refutation of all other alternatives and then follow with your solution.

Here are some key guidelines based on readers' various biases:

For the Uninterested Outsider

- Get attention with a startling discovery, striking question, pertinent quote, or prevalent problem.
- Offer your conclusions and/or recommendations.
- Present your supporting arguments in order of the most-important to the least-important points.
- Outline the cost and implementation plans, if appropriate.
- Refute alternative explanations or plans of action.

For example:

Our newest machine can save you 38 percent on . . .
The equipment's primary function is to . . .
The most important benefit is . . .
A second saving involves . . .
A third consideration will be . . .
We can install it in 48 hours for X dollars . . .
Neither the X machine nor the Y machine equals the
    precision of . . .

For the Interested but
Unbiased Internal Reader

- State your conclusions and/or recommendations.
- Present your supporting arguments in order of the most-important to the least-important evidence.
- Outline the cost and implementation plans.
- Refute alternative explanations or actions.

For example:

Our field tests indicate that the new machine has the capacity
    to . . . and I recommend . . .
Important test #1 showed . . .
Less-important test #2 revealed . . .
Test #3 also verified that . . .
The costs will involve . . . and I recommend that we begin
    phase 1 in the second quarter under the direction of . . .
Earlier questions (problems) that can now be put aside are
    . . .

For the Interested but Biased Reader

- Raise a striking question or pertinent problem.
- Suggest and then refute alternative explanations, conclusions, and/or recommendations.
- Present your conclusions and/or recommendations.
- Outline the cost and implementation plans.

For example:

Is it possible to . . . ?
The most obvious answer seems to be . . . but that won't
  explain the problem with . . .
Another plausible solution would be to . . . but neither will
  that overcome the . . .
A third course of action might be to . . . but that will cause
  serious difficulties with . . .
Therefore, my conclusion (recommendation) is . . .
The project will require X dollars in 19— to begin phase 1,
  which involves . . .

If you do not attempt to control the reasoning of readers but instead simply present your facts, they may agree with each fact you present and still arrive at a totally different conclusion. (See **Figure 4–3** on page 27 for an illustration of this danger.)

Persuasive writing requires structuring your report or proposal around your audience's interests and biases.

11.2 What Is Persuasive Language?

Persuasion involves knowing your reader's needs, wants, and values and offering to meet those needs or support those values. Persuasive language is not hyperbole, mysterious sources, vague qualifiers and hedging, name-calling, oversimplification, facts presented as reasons, or begging the question.

The preceding section established that all technical writers must at times be persuasive. To many writers, however, that means exaggeration and braggadocio and lots of superlatives.

Such writing will not necessarily be persuasive to a reader. Consider the following example, which is filled with high-flown language:

Our system has been **widely tested** in its **exceptional** capabilities to provide the **most up-to-date** search capacity, the **most thorough** cross-referencing capabilities, and **unsurpassed** workmanship on terminal design.

In proposal writing, the essence of persuasion is knowing exactly what your reader values, wants, or needs and then presenting your information to meet those needs or support those values. (See **Figure 11–1** for an example of persuasive writing based on a reader's needs.) If your reader values accuracy, you will document the precision of your testing tools. If your reader values speed in production, you will emphasize how your solution quickly converts raw material into a finished product.

Persuasive writing also means emphasizing benefits rather than specifications or features. How will you solve the reader's problems? Why is this the best solution?

In a technical report, persuasive writing requires sound logic

---

Persuasive Writing

Subject: Recommendation to Purchase S/48 with Changes

In light of your criteria—that the system have high-speed print, full word-processing capabilities, and data-text merge—I propose that you purchase the S/48 system with the following changes:

- A 90-megabyte disk instead of a 40-megabyte disk
- Perfectwrite/48 instead of Text Write
- No communications software

The saving that results from deleting the communications software almost exactly offsets the cost of the additional changes. The total cost will be $85,640.

Other alternatives examined and rejected:

System	Limitation
Delta	No data-text merge
H/36	Much too slow in printing
Max 2	Data processing does not have index features

Figure 11–1. Persuasive writing. Facts interpreted to meet the reader's needs, not high-flown language, make documents persuasive.

and thorough research and interpretation. You add credibility to your work when you cite alternative methods for solving a problem or designing a model and then give reasons for your choice. Credibility also increases when you are careful to define what your process or design can and cannot do. In other words:

- don't ignore opposing views or options
- be straightforward
- prefer understatement to overstatement—let the reader develop his or her own enthusiasm for what you have to say

Note the approach of the following writer.

An alternative explanation: two clouds colliding. Besides collapse, the only other obvious interpretation of the data is that the star formation is the result of two clouds colliding along the line of sight. Although this possibility cannot be entirely ruled out, it is improbable. The two peaks in the CO (1-0) and CS (1-0) spectra are clearly due to self-absorption. Since there is no evidence for a spatial separation into two clouds in any of the data, the clouds would have to be well aligned along the line of sight, an unlikely special geometry. Note that the average velocity dispersion for molecular clouds in the galaxy is about 5 km sec^{-1}. The root-mean-square velocity for random collisions would then be about 7 km sec^{-1}. The difference between the average HCO$^+$ emission and absorption velocities in W49A is 13 km sec^{-1}, substantially greater than 7 km sec^{-1}, which means that a random collision is unlikely. Finally, in the cloud collision model, the foreground cloud velocities must, by coincidence, exactly mimic the free-fall collapse velocities. We favor the simpler collapse model that naturally explains the range of absorption velocities of the HCO$^+$ and other molecular lines as well as the observed cloud structure.[1]

On the other hand, an erroneous idea of what persuasive documents involve may weaken rather than strengthen your writing. Let's focus on what persuasive writing is *not*.

Hyperbole. Overstatement used for emphasis generally calls attention to the exaggeration rather than to the key point.

Stripping this field without use of our Model 238 will be much like trimming a lawn with scissors.

---

[1]William J. Welch et al., "Star Formation in W49A: Gravitational Collapse of the Molecular Cloud Core toward a Ring of Massive Stars," *Science* 238 (1987): 1553. Copyright 1987 by the AAAS. Reprinted by permission of author and publisher.

Often such hyperbole angers a thoughtful reader or one who is biased against your position.

Understatement, deliberate downplaying of the possibilities of your idea, can be much more effective in motivating a reader to champion your cause.

Mysterious sources. Common lead-ins to unsupported generalizations include such statements as these: "As leading experts will agree . . .," "A search of the literature reveals . . .," "Long known to industry experts . . .," "A leading representative of the field . . .," "Several professors at major universities . . . ." If you have a renowned source, identify that source. Hidden authorities, as in the following passage, invite readers to ignore, or at least be skeptical of, your idea.

> Some advanced thermoplastics and thermoplastic composites **are said** to have broken the processing-time barrier: one-minute cycle times are already possible, with **some resin producers** estimating 45-second part-to-part times in the near future. In addition, many of these materials **are said** to provide surface qualities better than those of alternative polymers and even steels. **Many believe** that these thermoplastics offer a number of inherently better qualities than RIMed urethanes and thermosets molded by today's technology. However, **some of the most ambitious predictions by the automakers** for thermoplastics usage through the earlier part of the next decade have been modified. Costs have not come down to expectations, **according to some users,** while **many observers** feel that these materials are simply too new to inspire needed confidence of **the automakers.**[2]

Vague qualifiers and hedging. Many writers fear someone will take their words out of context. Therefore, they add qualifiers and hedgers in every sentence nook and cranny. The overall result is wimpy writing. That is not to say that you should make absolute statements that are unsupportable. But do watch for unnecessarily vague weasel words and hedgers.

For example, note the wishy-washy effect of the following statements (hedgers and qualifiers are in bold face):

> The paint **should** resist dust and **should** reduce maintenance costs **significantly.**

---

[2]"The Big Body-Panel Debate," *Advanced Materials and Processes Inc. Metal Progress,* May 1987, p. 56. Reprinted by permission of publisher.

It should be **strongly** emphasized that the **probability** of a **worst-case situation** occurring is **apparently very low.**

Listed below are **suggested possible** courses of action that **appear** to warrant **further consideration.**

On most occasions, the regulator meets the criteria established by our research team; however, **possible deviations may suggest** that NRC reevaluate the decision to modify our **current needs.**

Name-calling. Calling the competitor's research, product, or service "insignificant," "intolerable," or "primitive" doesn't make it so. Refuting option A does not necessarily lead the reader to embrace option B, which you favor. In fact, criticism of another's work can set your own work up for closer scrutiny than you desire. It is better simply to offer your work to your readers and let it speak for itself.

Oversimplification. Simple answers to complex problems are tools of politicians. This fact no doubt explains their shoddy record at actually solving problems. No, we don't mean that readers dislike simple solutions; but oversimplification invites skepticism and makes the knowledgeable reader doubt the writer's understanding of the situation.

Calling something simple doesn't make it so. You need as much evidence and explanation to support a simple answer as for a complex one—maybe more.

Facts presented as reasons. Don't confuse facts with reasons. To be persuasive, facts need interpretation.

Why should we offer the lab supply business a sole-source contract? (1) Vendor A will give us a 15 percent discount as our sole-source contractor. (2) Vendor B has had difficulty filling our chemical orders from the Lafayette lab. (3) Vendor C has been doing business with our competitors for the past eight years.

None of the above facts by itself is a reason for awarding the sole-source contract to vendor A. We can't evaluate the 15 percent discount until we compare it to the prices of vendors B and C. Vendor B's difficulty in filling orders has nothing to do with vendor A's or vendor C's ability to fill orders. And Vendor C may or may not have a conflict of interest in dealing with us and our competitors.

One of the biggest weaknesses in persuasive writing is the tendency to present facts without interpreting them in light of the question at hand. Facts are not reasons.

For example, let's say Fred's company is considering getting into the pen or into the pencil business, and the president has asked him to evaluate the potential of the two kinds of products and determine which would be the most profitable to manufacture and sell. Fred's key points might be as follows:

- Inks come in a variety of colors.
- Pens are good for signing legal documents.
- Pens are cylindrical and lightweight.

Fred concludes, let's manufacture and sell pens.

But why? The listed statements do not support the conclusion. Perhaps the argument is in the writer's head, but it's not on the page. Yes, pen ink comes in many colors, but so does pencil lead. And what does a variety of colors have to do with bottom-line profits? Is the writer saying that the variety of colors will attract more buyers? But readers might also conclude that the inventory and start-up costs would have to be greater with a variety of ink colors.

And as far as the usefulness in signing legal documents, what if only one out of every 1,000 documents written by the customer is a legal document? That "benefit" is really of little value.

Finally, what does their cylindrical shape and weight have to do with their manufacturing and marketing? Should Fred's company improve on that design? Retain the customary shape and weight? Or make a heavier, square pen instead?

Many scientific writers assume that "the facts speak for themselves." Rarely is that the case. Facts and evidence need interpretation. When that interpretation is not evident on the page, the reader stumbles over the gaps in logic.

Begging the question.   Begging the question involves talking around the issue without addressing it. Technical writers beg the question with great pronouncements such as these:

I suggest users perform these tests quarterly because the results will give them further information.

The steel frame was lowered to the seabed because we placed it immediately above the remains of the hull.

The salvage consultants determined that we should reinforce the welded joints because this was the wisest preventive solution.

More testing may be useful because it may shed more light on the subject.

Persuasive language involves a logical presentation of facts and information, not a fanfare of fancy, overblown pronouncements that are trivially true.

12

Passive Style
Versus Direct Style

12.1   Do Technical Writers Have a Writing Style?

Technical specialists establish their credibility in two ways: (1) with their facts, evidence, and logic and (2) with their writing style. A heavy, academic writing style will not camouflage the fact that a report has nothing important to say. And even good ideas will not travel well when mired in ponderous prose. The mark of a good technical writer is the ability to express a complex idea in a style simple and direct enough for a lay audience to understand.

Your writing style becomes a personal logo. And just as a company's logo consists of artwork, colors, and their arrangement, your writing style has three parts:

- The way you structure your ideas
- The illustrations you select to make your ideas clear and memorable
- The language you use

Other sections of this book deal with the first two parts of style; this section will focus on use of language.

A passive style, though perhaps difficult to define, is nevertheless easy to recognize. Those who write in a passive style bury the meat of their ideas in passive verbs. They select weak sentence subjects. They bury key actions. They add unnecessary qualifiers and intensifiers to vague abstractions. Finally, they drape their ideas in trite, verbose statements. Compare the following two writing styles:

Passive, Indirect Style:

> It can easily be seen that when large volumes of gas are metered and when there are variations in the gas temperatures, there is going to be a loss of revenue if some correcting device is not used.

Direct Style:

> As large volumes of gas are metered, gas temperature variation will result in lost revenues unless a correcting device is used.

Passive, Indirect Style:

Provided herewith is a report on the remainder of the findings with regard to the Unit #3 turbine. The contents should
be consistent with your present requirements, but if further
clarification is required, please advise.

Direct Style:

I've enclosed the report on the remainder of the findings
on the Unit #3 turbine. If you need further clarification,
please let me know.

Passive, Indirect Style:

It should be noted that the results of the Powell #3 workover
could change the rankings of the alternative courses of action. Therefore, no further action will be taken toward implementing Case D until the results of this workover are
assessed.

Direct Style:

Please note that the results of the Powell #3 workover could
change the rankings of the alternative courses of action.
Therefore, the Sewind group will take no further action toward implementing Case D until you have assessed these
results.

Passive, Indirect Style:

Structured maps which have been contoured on the top of
the Blaxton and San Matthews are shown in Figures 3A and
3B, respectively. Similarities exist between the structures of
the two zones, with both being elongated carbonate build-
ups with the axes following an east-to-west direction. It should
be noted that the structures of both zones decline drastically
toward the west and along the northern and southern flanks.
At the points of structural change, sections located in the
lower parts of the San Matthews can be said to become
progressively less productive.

Direct Style:

Figures 3A and 3B are structure maps contoured on the top
of the Blaxton and San Matthews, respectively. The structures of the two zones are similar. Both are elongated carbonate build-ups with east-to-west axes. Also both zones
drop toward the west and along their northern and southern

flanks. As the San Matthews changes, lower sections of the structure become progressively less productive.

What makes the first style indirect and passive and the second style direct is the subject of the following sections.

12.2   Negative News

Some writers choose a passive style when they have bad news or when they fear their readers will oppose their conclusions or recommendations. A passive style buries key points and tends to hedge. Writers with a direct style state any results of value, but also point out any failures.

You may have heard the story of the engineer who began his report this way: "We've just recently discovered one more way not to improve our bridge design."

Although this engineer had perhaps taken optimism to the extreme, technical professionals often find ways of placing negative results in a positive light. Many writers tend to view readers as inherently hostile and ready to pounce on them at the least bit of disappointing news or for unorthodox recommendations.

But you should not make such an assumption about your readers out of hand. Disappointment in the outcome does not mean a reader will doubt or criticize your work or conclusions.

As long as your work is valid, you should be just as direct and positive in your presentation as when the results are good. Hedging and qualifying bad news tend to detract from credibility.

Negative:

> We have no definite list of persons who will be assisting with the program conversion and no specific times of their availability [problem]; therefore, the staff will have difficulty in gaining access to the building [problem].

Positive:

> We have only a tentative list of persons who will be assisting with the program conversion and tentative schedules of their availability [problem]; therefore, the staff will need temporary ID's to gain access to the building [solution].

Negative:

> Under our present system, we manually attempt to override or accommodate the computer instructions [fact]. But the present method causes severe disruptions of the work flow [problem].

Positive:

> Under our present system, we manually override or accommodate the computer instructions [fact]. We can continue to function in this manner with some degree of effectiveness [implied problem]; however, certain changes will improve our system and minimize disruptions to the work flow [solution].

12.3 Active Voice Versus Passive Voice

Active verbs make your writing direct, clear, and concise. Passive verbs can add variety to your writing, soften commands, place emphasis on results when the doer is unimportant, help doers escape accountability, and slow the pace of your writing. Unless you have one of these reasons for using the passive voice, prefer active voice.

In sentences in the active voice, the subject performs the action. In sentences in the passive voice, the subject receives the action.

Passive:

> The study was completed by our investigators.

Active:

> Our investigators completed the study.

Passive:

> The design of such systems is simplified by the use of hydraulics.

Active:

> The use of hydraulics simplifies the design of such systems.

Passive:

> The significance of the makeup and test procedure on the leak resistance of API 8-round connectors is evaluated by a tool that extends the size range from 7 inches to 16 inches.

Active:

> A tool that extends the size range from 7 inches to 16 inches evaluates the significance of the makeup and test procedure on the leak resistance of API 8-round connectors.

Passive:

> Metallurgical analyses were performed by Brighton, Inc.

Active:

> Brighton, Inc. performed metallurgical analyses.

Active Verbs Are Direct

Passive:

> It has been suggested that the project be abandoned. (Who suggested it? Abandoned by whom?)

Active:

> R&D suggests that Weldon Associates abandon the project.

Passive:

> It is recommended that, while the meter is disassembled, a few drops of light instrument oil be placed in the bearings of the magnetic drive shaft.

Active:

> While the meter is disassembled, place a few drops of light instrument oil in the bearings of the magnetic drive shaft.

Active Verbs Are Clear

Passive:

> New personnel and budget resources have been promised to be committed to well completions in the lower subzones. (Who made this promise?)

Active:

> The TRW division has promised to commit new personnel and budget resources to well completions in the lower subzones.

Passive:

> The feasibility of extracting bitumen from tar sand with a patented hot water/solvent process will be assessed. (Who will assess it?)

Active:

> Our staff will assess the feasibility of extracting bitumen from tar sand with a patented hot water/solvent process.

Active Verbs Are Concise

Passive:

> The two main bearings can be lubricated by means of the external container [13 words].

Active:

> The external container can lubricate the two main bearings [9 words].

Passive:

> If coasting time has failed to reach the charted times, tests must be performed to determine where the increased frictional load has occurred [24 words].

Active:

> If coasting time has not reached the charted times, test the meter to determine the source of increased frictional load [20 words].

Passive:

> This mechanical output is connected to an electrical output by means of the pulse generator [15 words].

Active:

> The pulse generator connects the mechanical output to the electrical output [11 words].

The passive voice does, however, have a place in technical writing.

Passive Verbs Add Variety

We placed a viscous, saponified thixotropic crude in the annular space. Next, we preinsulated the injection string with calcium silicate. Then we insulated a concentric injection string that had been in use earlier. Finally, the production casing **was prestressed** in all wells.

Passive Verbs Soften Commands

The operation of the plotter **should be** carefully **explained** to all users before the program **is initiated.** (It sounds demanding or authoritarian to say "You should carefully explain the operation of the plotter to all users before you begin the program.")

Passive Verbs Emphasize Results When the Doer Is Unimportant or Unknown

Eighteen types of structures **have been encountered** in the 54 producing acres of the highly faulted Bengli region. (Who encountered them is unimportant.)

Passive Verbs Allow Doers to Escape Accountability

A quality and location differential of the crude oil **will be established** to force the buyer to proceed with the acquisition. (This downplays the issue of who will force the buyer.)

The format commands **were programmed** incorrectly. (This is less accusatory than "You programmed the commands incorrectly.")

Passive Verbs Slow the Pace of Your Writing

The development of the ROV has not been continuous. Several years elapsed before we recognized and exploited the potential of the original model. This hiatus **was** profitably **filled** by diving contractors, who began testing equipment and techniques to improve human endurance in progressively deeper waters, so extending a human's range from dives using simple air diving equipment at 32 or 65 feet to routine commercial dives with mixed breathing gases beyond 984 feet.

Unless you have one of the above-mentioned reasons for using the passive voice, prefer active verbs to make your writing direct, clear, and concise.

12.4 Buried Verbs, Buried Subjects, Buried Action

Don't bury important information by turning verbs into noun phrases or by using empty sentence beginnings such as **There are, There were, It is,** *or* **It was.**

We will assume you did good work. Okay, excellent work. Now you want to see some changes or some decisions, right? If so, don't suffocate your message or recommendations with weak subjects or verbs.

A verb expresses what a subject is, does, or has. Every English sentence has a verb, and verbs are what give sentences life. Yet some writers shy away from using strong, vivid verbs and instead turn them into nouns and noun phrases, making their sentences longer and duller.

In the sentences that follow, note the verbs that have been replaced by noun phrases and other clutter (in boldface).

Cluttered:

> **The discovery of** the Hawkrider Field was a major factor in **the production of** and **the distribution of** the product being done so inexpensively.

Strong:

> The Hawkrider discovery enabled us to produce and distribute the product so inexpensively.

Cluttered:

> **Additional analyses were performed** with estimates provided by Chicago **for the purpose of the identification of** supply costs and print volumes **that would** significantly affect the results.

Strong:

> With estimates from Chicago, we analyzed the figures to identify the supply costs and print volumes significantly affecting the results.

Cluttered:

> **The review of** the conversion program should be done first **from the overall point of view of the verification of** the whole chain.

Strong:

> Review the conversion program first to verify the whole chain.

Another way to take the punch out of a sentence is to give it a false subject. That is, some writers begin sentences with a mundane *there is, there are, there was, there were, it is,* or *it was* rather than the true subject.

Weak:

> There is a recent exception to the assumption of subsea maintenance, Jabiru No. 2A.

Improved:

> Jabiru No. 2A is a recent exception to the assumption of subsea maintenance.

Weak:

> There were two systems on board, each housed in a separate cage for over-the-side deployment.

Improved:

> The two systems on board were each housed in a separate cage for over-the-side deployment.

Weak:

> It is always very important to establish methods and procedures to determine that all metering is done accurately.

Improved:

> Establish methods and procedures to ensure that all metering is accurate.

Weak:

> It can be seen that the temperature effects are negligible.

Improved:

> The temperature effects are negligible.

Give your sentences life. Sentences that begin with their "real" subjects and use active verbs add impact to your ideas.

12.5   *I, We, One,* and the Disappearing Writer

Use personal pronouns when you need them to be clear.
Objectivity involves much more than third-person prose.

In teaching technical writing, we hear no question more often than "What about using personal pronouns? In school, we were taught to avoid *I, we,* and *you.* Doesn't the writing sound more objective without them?"

Objectivity has little to do with the use of pronouns. An editorial in the *Wall Street Journal* might use no personal pronouns, but certainly you realize you're not getting an unbiased opinion. Writers show objectivity (or lack of objectivity) by the facts they choose to include or to omit, by their choice of subject, by their sampling and testing procedures, and by their conclusions. Writing style and the use of personal pronouns is altogether different from scientific objectivity.

Note the use of personal pronouns in this passage from *The New England Journal of Medicine* (boldface added):

> **Our** findings concerning the overall incidence of acute and chronic GVHD are not appreciably different from those of other groups. Patients with Grades 0 through II acute GVHD fared better than those with more severe involvement, the latter group having a higher incidence of fatal infection. In this series, **we** found no association between acute GVHD and a reduced risk of posttransplantation relapse. However, as in other recent reports, **we** did find an association between the presence of chronic GHVD and a low relapse rate.[1]

When you're talking about work you did, *I* or *we* is perfectly proper. The ubiquitous *the authors* and *the writers* sound pompous, stuffy, and distant. Of course you wouldn't say *we* if you're speaking only for yourself rather than as a representative of a team or an organization. In general, state theories or facts in the third person; report your work as if you did it.

Outside of these two considerations, let clarity and effectiveness be your guide.

---

[1] Excerpted from material originally appearing in Joel A. Brochstein et al., "Allogeneic Bone Marrow Transplantation after Hyperfractionated Total-Body Irradiation and Cyclophosphamide in Children with Acute Leukemia," *The New England Journal of Medicine* 317 (1987): 1623. Reprinted by permission of publisher.

12.6 Hedging: Qualifiers, Intensifiers, Vague Abstractions

Hedging weakens the impact of your writing. Qualifiers, intensifiers, and vague abstractions overshadow key ideas.

Just as nature abhors a vacuum, engineers abhor a situation in which they might be pinned down to a black-and-white, this-or-that answer. We know that God ordained and set in motion a universe of great precision. Yet when we mortals try to measure and describe it, we are beset with nagging inconsistencies. Thus, we become equivocators, hedgers, and weaselers. We squirm because we know that if we're too specific, someone may come along later and prove us wrong. We vividly imagine ourselves standing before the ranks of our peers and having our badge of office, the plastic vest-pocket pencil holder, summarily ripped out after our slide rule snaps across the knee of the commandant. We are left to wander as forlorn and pitiful objects of scorn.

In the face of this predicament, equivocation becomes insurance. Hedging makes our position fluid enough to flow with future findings. In technical terms, the viscosity of the position is inversely proportional to the number of weasel words in the statement. Who among us has not encountered the "expert" who knew so much he or she couldn't answer a question?

On the other hand, you'll be quick to point out, simplistic solutions frequently emanate from simple minds. How, then, does one reach that balance between cowardly hedging and unsupported hype? State your points as emphatically as you can support them. No more, no less. If you're not sure, don't hedge. Simply state your level of uncertainty and the reasons behind it as straightforwardly as possible. Management will love you. Your peers will respect you.

To be sure, though, hedging does have its place; its value is limitless if you need to cover weaknesses in effort or logic. During the first technical writing workshop for the research and development section of a client company, a participant brought us the following "glossary of terms," saying that if we wanted to work for his company, we'd have to learn to interpret its reports:

It has long been known . . . (Translation: I haven't bothered to look up the original reference.)

Of great theoretical and practical importance . . . (Translation: Interesting to me.)

Three of the samples were chosen for detailed study. (Translation: The results of the others didn't make sense so we ignored those.)

Typical results are shown. (Translation: The best results are shown.)

These results will be reported at a later date. (Translation: I might get around to this sometime.)

An exhaustive review of recent literature shows . . . (Translation: I found a 1962 paper that says . . .)

It is believed that . . . (Translation: I think.)

It is generally believed that . . . (Translation: A couple of other people think so, too.)

It is clear that much additional work will be required before a complete understanding . . . (Translation: I don't understand it.)

Thanks are due to Joe Glotz for assistance with the experiment and to John Doe for valuable discussions. (Translation: Glotz did the work and Doe explained what it meant.)

The original author of this list is unknown, but he or she evidently had been reading the same kind of reports we see.

Hedging and vague abstractions abound everywhere—even in sales. A third-party investigator of investment real estate brought us a copy of his standard report for clients who ask him to inspect property before they buy it. In a four-page client report, five disclaimers insist that the investor should make his or her own decision about purchase of the property because all investigative findings presented in the report are based on "appearance."

When we suggested that the investigator add only one blanket disclaimer at the end of the report, he grew concerned that it wouldn't be "enough." The disclaimers were equivalent to saying "Don't count on this report—I'm not standing by anything at all that it might say." And this report was intended to be a sales tool!

So what to do if you have qualifications to make? At the outset, state clearly the scope of your work, the specifications, and the assumptions. Then be straightforward in your conclusions and recommendations. If you're not sure about a point, say so. Some of the qualifiers, intensifiers, and vague abstractions found most often in

---

Qualifiers, Intensifiers, Vague Abstractions

Qualifiers

to some degree	rather	primarily
to some extent	tolerable	largely
reasonably	generally	may possibly
considerable	commonly	perhaps
appears	seems	apparently
more or less	significantly	should be

Intensifiers

very	purely	well under
absolutely	especially	well over
so	genuinely	completely
quite	extremely	simply

Vague Abstractions

various factors (scheduling? personnel? money?)
several approaches (to an airport runway?)
similar types (similar in cost? in materials?)
facilities (warehouses? toilets?)
units (pencils? lots? buildings?)
in this manner
in this mode
in this fashion
has various capabilities to
quite a few
a number of
a small amount
a significant amount

Figure 12–1. Qualifiers, intensifiers, and vague abstractions. Be straightforward and confident in your writing. Hedging and vague qualifiers overshadow key ideas.

technical writing are included in **Figure 12–1.** Remember that human nature leads us to interpret vague words and phrases negatively. Additionally, such writing sounds unclear and dull and suggests the writer is afraid to take a stand.

12.7   Strong and Simple Versus Bland and Complex

Precise, simple words will make your writing powerful.

It is often said that API standards compose the "Bible" for the conduct of business in the oil patch. There is a certain truth to this idea: Everyone considers it sacred literature, but no one seems to read it.[2]

Although a humorous analogy makes a memorable point, colorful writing does not require you to be a comic in your reports and correspondence. Colorful writing does, however, mean that you select words, expressions, and figures of speech that add impact to your ideas.

Use big words only when there's no small word with the same meaning or when you purposely want to confuse your reader. As soon as a trendy word is coined, it's on its way to becoming a cliché. Instead of making your writing colorful, such clichés make it trite.

An engineer once brought us a draft of a memo he had been struggling to write for two days. After reading it, we commented that it sounded fine, that it was both clear and concise. "Yeah," he responded, "but it just doesn't sound businesslike—I have a hard time writing in a businesslike style."

Anyone who's laboring under the false impression that "businesslike," "technical," "official," or "objective" means using the longest sentences and the biggest words possible can relax. Readers are impressed by ideas and the work they represent, not a heavy academic writing style that puts even the most interested and intelligent to sleep.

Unfortunately, some technical writers work hard to turn simple, strong words into bland, complex substitutes (see **Figure 12–2**).

Bland writing means unnecessarily big words and clichés that make all of your documents sound as though they're written on a computer with limited disk space. Words and phrases that easily slide onto your page are probably clichés that need to be replaced by more precise, up-to-date terms (see **Figure 12–3**).

A comparison of the bland and the colorful can be illustrated better than explained:

---

[2]T.H. Hill et al., "Qualifying Drillstring Components for Deep Drilling," *Journal of Petroleum Technology*, August 1985, p. 1512. Reprinted by permission of publisher.

Bland, Complex Writing Versus
Strong, Simple Writing

Complex	Simple
aggregate	sum, total, whole
anomalous	unusual
antithesis	opposite
abbreviate	condense
cessation	stop, end
cognizant	aware
commencement	beginning
concept	idea
conjecture	guess
demonstrate	show
disengage	free
duplicate	copy
elucidate	clarify
enumerate	number, list
facilitate	help
homogeneous	like, similar
implement, implementation	put into use, use
impairment	harm, damage
incision	cut
incombustible	fireproof
initiate	begin
methodology	methods, procedure
modify, modification	change
miniscule	tiny
opine	think
optimum	best
subsequent	next
sufficient	enough
terminate	end
utilize	use
verification	check, proof

Figure 12–2. Bland, complex writing versus strong, simple writing. The key to strong, lucid prose is simplicity.

Technical Clichés

state of the art

advanced technology

applied research

prioritize

bottom line

status quo

relevant

meaningful

significant reduction (increase)

viable alternative

at this point in time

under consideration

under separate cover

under review

vitally important

boilerplate

gold plated

rubber-stamped

not invented here

a search of the literature

Figure 12–3. Technical clichés. Clichés indicate lazy thinking.

Strong, Simple, Colorful:

The effects of the ultraviolet waves are much more violent than are those of the visible and infrared—excessive exposure to ultraviolet can cause a severe burn and damage to the lens of the eye with no warning whatsoever. Electric welding arcs and germicidal lamps are the most common

large producers of ultraviolet in industry. The ordinary flu-
orescent lamp generates ultraviolet inside the bulb, but it is
almost entirely absorbed by the bulb and its coating. The
most common exposure to ultraviolet radiation is from direct
sunlight, which can result in sunburn. Also, while most people have become familiar with certain compounds and lo-
tions that minimize the effects of the sun's rays, many are
unaware that some industrial materials, such as cresols, make
the skin especially sensitive to ultraviolet rays. So much so
that even short exposure results in severe sunburn.

• • •

Because of the long cable lengths, the preferred method of
installation is center pulling. The cable reel, placed at an
intermediate point, is pulled into the conduit. The remainder
of the cable is then removed from the reel, laid out in a
figure eight pattern to preclude kinking, and pulled by the
other end into the second conduit. The advantages of this
installation method are a reduced crew size and fewer blow-
ers and trucks.

• • •

Generally, text and graphic scanners use one of two methods
to capture a page. Some systems transport paper past a window that illuminates the line and projects it onto a charged
couple device (CCD), while others move the optics over a
fixed scanning bed. Both methods require precise mechanical tolerances, particularly for text scanning. A 1-pixel error
per line can trigger an entire page of unrecognized and unwanted characters.

Bland:

The engineering contractor and subcontractors must spon-
sor the development of a modification design concept which
permits all field work and activities on the dock and dolphins
to be broken into periods of 48 hours. At the conclusion of
each successive 48-hour task, the original mooring capabilities of the facility (utilizing existing and/or new state-of-the-
art equipment) must be in a state of restoration. The 48-hour
period additionally encompasses any periods of time required for mobilization or demobilization activities and tasks
related to the contractual specifications contained herein.

13

Technical Accuracy
and Completeness

> *Avoid vague, unsupported generalizations. Identify subjective statements as such. Use numbers, statistics, and symbols with care, and be as technically precise as necessary for your intended audience.*

Is it really necessary to emphasize accuracy and precision to scientists, engineers, data processors, and other technical professionals? A story about IBM should suffice as answer: "When I first came to work for the company, I was asked to sit in on a meeting in which my boss was making a big presentation to his bosses. On about the fifth slide, one of the VPs in the group said, 'Back up. That figure doesn't agree with the one you had on the second slide.' My boss went back to the previous slide and found the discrepancy. The VP's comment was, 'Sit down. Everything you say from now on will be totally invalid for me.' I remember thinking at the time that he was awfully harsh and rude for that kind of mistake. But . . . I don't know. . . . I see his point now that I'm a manager myself. I get so tired of seeing reports with errors—just carelessness and sloppiness. They really affect credibility."

Similar stories about technical inaccuracies surface frequently. Check your own writing for the following weaknesses, which have no place in technical documents.

Avoid vagueness; quantify when you can. Be precise and diligent in presenting the details and statistics necessary for your intended audience and for your purpose. Vagueness can lead to misunderstanding and may cast doubt on all your research.

Not: Several prior studies . . .
But: Three prior studies . . .

Not: A large number of well completions . . .
But: Almost 1200 well completions . . .

Not: We spent several weeks investigating whether . . .
But: We spent 24 days investigating whether . . .

Not: A majority of our lab samples . . .
But: Eighty percent of our lab samples . . .

Beware of unsupported generalizations. When you feel the need to make statements such as the following, beware of the tendency to write your "facts" rather than research them.

As leading experts have noted . . . (Who? Where?)
Few will doubt . . . (If that's true, why point it out?)
Few will argue with the fact that . . . (An attempt to keep me
  from arguing?)
Most scientists writing at that time . . . (What survey?)
The vast majority of engineers today . . . (Agree? You've got
  to be kidding.)
Several professors at major universities . . . (Your graduate
  advisor and who else?)

Identify subjective statements as such.   When scientists pile fact
upon fact, readers may become lazy; they may accept unsupported,
subjective statements along with the rest. Therefore, it's the technical
writer's responsibility to warn readers when there could be other
plausible interpretations of a finding or other conclusions drawn from
test results.

Use direct statements to identify subjective, controversial comments rather than hedge words and phrases:

Although others may differ in their interpretations of these
findings, I believe . . .

Although some may argue that . . ., I propose . . .

It is my opinion that . . .

I think . . .

In my estimation, the results show . . .

While there are other feasible alternatives, my work suggests
that . . .

Use numbers, statistics, and symbols with care.   If there's one com-
monality of most technical writing, it's a document chockful of jargon,
symbols, abbreviations, and numbers. If the subject is already a complex one, the numbers and symbols add to its complexity. Therefore,
handle all numbers, statistics, and symbols with care.

Some of the most insidious misusers of "statistics" are the writers
of television commercials. By no means will we call them technical
writers, but they do offer several examples of misleading statistics.

A few years ago when smaller imported cars were first gaining
popularity, reliability became a key consumer issue. At that time, the
following claim appeared on national television: "Nine out of ten
Volvos sold in this country during the last ten years are still on the
road."

This message left the impression of a phalanx of battered but
indomitable Volvos, with an average age of five years, still faithfully

serving their owners. What the commercial failed to mention was this: Volvos, and imports in general, were enjoying an unprecedented surge in popularity in America. Therefore, nine out of ten Volvos sold in this country during the previous ten years were probably sold during the previous 12–24 months. All Volvos more than two years old could have been in the junkyard and the "statistic" would still have been correct!

Scientists, engineers, and other technical professionals normally do not purposefully mislead. But carelessness with statistics can confuse readers.

In the testing and procedural sections of a report, of course, you will give numbers that are appropriately precise because readers of these sections will need to know specifics. But when you summarize the major conclusions in an executive overview, be cautious about statistical overkill. Rounded numbers are easier to grasp quickly and to remember ("about 50 percent" rather than "51.1 percent").

Keep these additional guidelines in mind:

- Express decimal numbers using significant digits—and no more.
- Always use the same basis for comparisons.
- Always specify the base in any expression of percentages.
- Introduce acronyms and symbols before using them. (For example: Quality assurance (QA) is . . .)
- Define all symbols unfamiliar to any of your readers.
- Follow grammatical rules to fit symbols substituting for words into a sentence.
- Center equations on separate lines in the text and keep all fractions and signs on the same level. (Exceptions, of course, include numerators, denominators, and exponents)
- Express units of measurement by using words or standard symbols, not informal abbreviations.

Part 3

Guidelines
for Specific
Documents

14

Formal Research Reports

14.1   Title and Title Page

Title pages, balanced and uncrowded, should contain vital information. Report or article titles should be descriptive enough to allow accurate abstracting for other researchers. Eliminate title deadwood: the obvious, the general, and the vague. The title and abstract fit together as a unit; therefore, the title should not be repeated verbatim in the abstract.

The purpose of a title page is not to be a cover sheet; a blank white page would do nicely for that. To serve its appropriate function, a title page should look balanced and uncrowded and include the following:

- Title of report
- The code, contract, or project number, if any
- Author(s) of report and affiliation
- Where presented or to whom submitted
- Date of submission or presentation
- The security or confidentiality notice, if any

All of these pieces of information belonging on a title page are as easy to prepare as hitting keys on a keyboard—except the title.

An effective title may take hours of thought. Publishers routinely go through agony over book and article titles to be splashed on front covers. An effective title can sell a mediocre book and a poor title can hide a potential bestseller. To authors and publishers, effective titles mean big bucks.

But you as a technical writer have much more at stake than dollars. Your research may be lost to the scientific world altogether if your title is so ineffective that it gets no attention or if it is too vague to be appropriately abstracted for further research. Such is the case in company archives as well as professional abstracting services. Much research is duplicated simply because titles and abstracts are so poorly written that no one can retrieve the information hidden within them. Can you imagine how an abstracting service listed the reports carrying these titles?

Diet and Cancer
Artificial Chromosomes
Laboratory Antarctica: Research Contributions to Global Problems

So how do you write an effective title?

The title should distinguish your report from all others. What about your study makes it unique? Whatever it is, you should somehow include it in your title. Generally, the more specific your investigation has been, the more words it will take to describe it clearly.

Dry-Coupled Ultrasonic Elasticity Measurements of Sintered Ceramics and Their Green States

Quantitative Flaw Characterization with Scanning Laser Acoustic Microscopy

Blocking of HIV-1 Infectivity by a Soluble, Secreted Form of the CD4 Antigen

MWD Monitoring of Gas Kicks Ensures Safer Drilling

Potassium/Lime Drilling-Fluid System in Navarin Basin Drilling

Fatal Thrombotic Disorder Associated with an Acquired Inhibitor of Protein C

Filtration Method Characterizes Dispersive Properties of Shales

Evidence for Divergent Plate-Boundary Characteristics and Crustal Spreading on Venus

Human Proto-Oncogene c-jun Encodes a DNA Binding Protein with Structured and Functional Properties of Transcription Factor AP-1

Flow Distribution in a Roller Jet Bit Determined from Hot-Wire Anemometry Measurements

Because you need so many precise, descriptive words to set your research apart, you should eliminate all deadwood (the obvious, the unnecessary, the general):

A History of . . .
The Use of . . .
A Study of . . .
A Report on . . .
An Investigation into . . .
Various Aspects of . . .
Several Approaches to . . .
Various Techniques of . . .
An Analysis of the Performance of . . .

Finally, consider your title and abstract as a unit. Rarely will readers see one without the other. Therefore, try not to repeat the title verbatim in your opening abstract statement.

14.2 Table of Contents

A table of contents should be specific, informative, and easily accessible.

The table of contents is the key to the functionality of reports and proposals; it is not window dressing. The table of contents

- directs senior executives to the most important information
- directs other skimming readers to specific technical sections
- overviews the scope and contents of the report
- highlights key ideas
- helps readers relocate information.

Therefore, items in the table of contents should be as informative as possible. That is, don't settle for unimaginative listings such as *Introduction, Scope, Conclusions, Recommendations,* and *Procedures.*

If you do use these general categories, then provide more specific subheadings. In addition to a generic *Advantages,* give a capsule phrase of each advantage:

Advantages
    Increased Accuracy in Reporting
    Higher Pain Threshold
    Subdued Melting

In addition to a generic *Recommendations,* give a capsule phrase of what you propose:

Recommendations
    Telecommunications for Cyber Processing
    Telecommunications for Remote Users
    Interface to Manufacturing Process Control
    Network Monitoring
    Replacement of S/377

Put yourself in the reader's place and consider which of the tables of contents shown in **Figure 14-1** would make the information more accessible.

Tables of Contents

Version 1: Vague, Uninformative Entries

Purpose
Environment
Specifications
Report Examples
Programs
Utilities

Version 2: Specific, Informative Entries

Purpose of the Proposed Documentation
   To Support the Safety Program
Purpose of the Proposed System
   To Input Monthly Safety Summaries at the Refineries
   To Calculate Statistics
   To Print Reports at Headquarters
Environment
   MXXC Computing Center
   User Restrictions
Specifications
   Database
   Screen
Programs
   Identifying Obsolete Equipment
   Modifying New Parts
   Securing Approvals and Authorizations
   Notifying All Users about Changes
   Initiating and Cancelling Orders
Report Examples
   Monthly Summaries
   Statistical Summaries at the Refineries
Programs
   Menu
   Input
Utilities
   Database
   Input

Figure 14–1. Tables of contents. A table of contents must be specific and informative to serve both the reader's and writer's purposes.

140

A table of contents should not include pages that precede it, such as a title page or a transmittal letter. But everything else in the report should be listed.

Finally, list the full titles of all tables and figures separately because readers will most frequently refer to these again and again.

Let accessibility be your guide. The table of contents, as a reading tool, should be functional.

14.3   Other Front Matter: Preface, Foreword, and Acknowledgments

The preface, foreword, and acknowledgments should not repeat the bibliographic or other introductory sections of your report. Rather, they should contain only highlights. Many readers will not read the front matter at all.

The preface or foreword is an introduction, usually by the author, that explains such things as the scope, the purpose, and the background of the document. A preface or foreword may also acknowledge those who helped in your work: your technical research staff; those with whom you discussed your findings, conclusions, and recommendations; those whose published works you have drawn from in your own research; and finally those who helped in manuscript preparation. Modesty wears well.

If other parts of your paper present your purpose, scope, and background, forego having a preface or foreword and cite those who helped in a section entitled *Acknowledgments*.

14.4   Abstract

Abstracts summarize new contributions to a field, provide key words for computer searches, establish a framework for the significance of an entire report, allow meeting attendees to select sessions to attend, and remind attendees or readers of what they've heard or read. Informative abstracts provide stand-alone summaries of key report information. Descriptive abstracts merely tell readers the general nature of the information they'll find

> *in the full report. Always prefer an informative abstract to a descriptive one.*

A key question we ask of a prospective client in order to customize a technical writing workshop is, Do your professionals write abstracts or executive summaries?

The client often gives us a puzzled look. "Well, . . . I don't know. I think it's probably a combination of the two or something in between. Give me your definitions and I'll see if what we do fits."

Our point is that there is much confusion about the terms *abstracts* and *executive summaries*. Some technical writers use the terms interchangeably; others outline differences. To clarify what you need to write for your job or for publication, we'll take our stand by defining them differently and presenting examples of each. Then you can decide which are required for your own projects.

Executive summaries

- provide information for decision makers or nontechnical audiences.
- give more attention to conclusions and recommendations than to procedure.
- may or may not follow the order of the report.
- run much longer than an abstract—sometimes several pages.

Abstracts

- provide information for technical audiences.
- follow the exact order of the full report.
- devote the same emphasis to each section that the full report does.
- usually run no more than 250 words.

A title and an abstract fit together as a unit; therefore, the title should not be repeated verbatim in the abstract. An abstract fulfills a vital function within a report. It

- summarizes new contributions to a field.
- provides key words for computer searches.
- establishes the framework for understanding the details and significance of the full report.
- allows meeting attendees to select sessions to attend.

- reminds attendees or readers of what they've heard or read.

Abstracts come in two varieties: the *descriptive* (sometimes called the *indicative*) and the *informative*.

Descriptive abstracts.   These read much like a table of contents in paragraph form. They focus on the development of the paper rather than on the key pieces of information. In other words, descriptive abstracts promise to tell you something informative—later, when you read the entire report. For example:

> This report will review an argument between John and Mary. It will explain how the argument began and the possible repercussions of that argument, should it not be settled at some later date. The attitudes of both Mary and John will be discussed and their decision to go their separate ways and pursue other interests will be analyzed. Recommendations about further relationships with other interested parties will be presented.

The readers of such abstracts always have questions. For example, what was the argument about? What was John's attitude? What was Mary's attitude? Why did they decide to go their separate ways? What are their "other interests" and "other relationships"?

So when do you use such promising, but noninformative, abstracts?

- When the results, conclusions, or recommendations are so numerous that they cannot be presented in brief abstract form.
- When you are presenting a paper orally and you don't want your audience to read your abstract, learn your secrets, and then skip your session. (Note: This situation works only if the paper was not published before the meeting.)

To develop a descriptive abstract, simply review your table of contents and turn your topics into sentences. However, never write a descriptive abstract when you can provide an informative one.

Informative Abstracts.   An informative abstract informs; it is the telegram version of the entire report (and can include quantitative information). For example:

> John and Mary had a major disagreement about how to spend the $2 million they won in a state lottery. John wanted to spend it on a condominium in Cancun, a private jet, and a trip to the Orient. Mary wanted to save the $2 million for

retirement at the age of 50. John secretly withdrew his half of the money, bought his jet, and landed on Ruth's rice paddy in the Orient. He forgot about Cancun. Angry at the deception, Mary withdrew her million dollars, hired a lawyer, and sued John for half his rice cakes. She and her lawyer retired to Cancun while waiting for the appeal to be heard by the Supreme Court.

Always prefer an informative abstract over a descriptive one. An informative abstract is clear and specific. It presents an accurate picture of the paper itself.

To develop an effective, informative abstract, review your informative headings and opening overview sentences under each heading. Select the most important points from each section, and prune away the less significant. Tell what was done, why it was done, and how it was done. Also include key findings and conclusions.

Note the differences between the following descriptive and informative abstracts:

Descriptive:

The functions of splices, connectors, and power couplers are reviewed. Parameters of interest to system designers are identified. The sources of loss in splices and connectors are summarized and typical loss values given. Specific designs of splices, connectors, and couplers for telecommunications and computer network applications are discussed.[1]

But the reader wants to know which of the functions are discussed. What are the parameters? What are the sources of loss and the typical loss values? What are the unique features of these specific designs?

Descriptive:

The relative positions of the centers of mass of the 21 proteins of the 30S ribosomal subunit from *Escherichia coli* have been determined by triangulation using neutron scattering data. The resulting map of the quaternary structure of the small ribosomal subunit is presented, and comparisons are made with structural data from other sources.[2]

---

[1]Jack F. Dalgleish, "Splices, Connectors, and Power Couplers for Field and Office Use," *Proceedings of the IEEE* 68 (1980): 1226. Copyright © 1980 IEEE. Reprinted by permission of publisher.

[2]M. S. Capel et al., "A Complete Mapping of the Proteins in the Small Ribosomal Subunit of *Escherichia Coli*," *Science* 238 (1987): 1403. Copyright 1987 by the AAAS. Reprinted by permission of publisher.

Although this abstract doesn't present the key information of interest—the structure of the small ribosomal subunit—such an informative abstract would be impossible to write for this kind of article. The map is the main interest.

Informative:

> Flawed parts representing a very small fraction of production can generate major percentages of downtime in automated assembly operations. In the example studied and resolved in this paper, a defect rate of 0.1 percent resulted in 50 percent downtime. The problem was resolved by installing an automatic nondestructive selection instrument to qualify the feed parts 100 percent. The principle of this acoustic noncontacting system is to envelop the entire part in a sonic field and analyze the resulting reflected sonic wave field for the presence of reflections not characteristic of good parts. The analysis is performed by artificial intelligence after the instrument is calibrated by letting it "learn" the characteristics of the wave field for good parts.
>
> The instrument is able to detect all the flaws present in any of the small stamped sheet metal parts used in the assembly in question, and to reject flawed parts. With its use, the downtime attributed to faulty feed parts has been reduced to less than 2 percent, and the production rate of the automated assembly machine has been increased to its design value. The acoustic instrument is versatile and can be recalibrated for other parts in a matter of minutes by "learning" their sonic characteristics. As in this case, where defect rates too small to treat by statistical process control are able to interfere severely with automated assembly, automated qualification of the parts by nondestructive means should be performed.[3]

Informative:

> The relatively nonspecific single-stranded deoxyribonuclease, staphylococcal nuclease, was selectively fused to an oligonucleotide binding site of defined sequence to generate a hybrid enzyme. A cysteine was substituted for Lys[116] in the

---

[3]Martha A. Glabicky-Fegan, "Elimination of Downtime in an Automated Assembly Operation by Nondestructive Qualification of Feed Parts," *Materials Evaluation*, November 1987, p. 311. Copyright© 1987, the American Society for Nondestructive Testing, Inc. Columbus, Ohio. Reprinted with permission from *Materials Evaluation*.

enzyme by oligonucleotide-directed mutagenesis and coupled to an oligonucleotide that contained a 3'-thiol. The resulting hybrid enzyme cleaved single-stranded DNA at sites adjacent to the oligonucleotide binding site.[4]

Informative:

The traditional view that quantal release of neurotransmitter results from the fusion of transmitter-containing vesicles with the neuronal membrane has been recently challenged. Although various alternative mechanisms have been proposed, a common element among them is the release of cytoplasmic transmitter, which, in one view, could occur through large conductance channels on the presynaptic membrane. Six nerve-muscle cell pairs were examined with a whole-cell patch clamp for the presence of such channels that are associated with the production of miniature end-plate potentials. Examination of the neuronal membrane current during the occurrence of 822 miniature end-plate potentials produced no evidence of large channels. Thus it is unlikely that quantal release is mediated by such channels in the neuromuscular junction.[5]

Informative abstracts present all the key information of a report or article; some readers can find all they need there and may never have to read the entire report. Even readers who want more detailed information can ascertain from such an informative abstract precisely what details they will find in the complete document.

14.5   Executive Summary

An executive summary is a report in miniature and therefore should present all key information. It is, however, generally addressed to nontechnical audiences. Executive summaries give more attention to conclusions and recommendations than to procedure, may or may not follow the order of the report, and run longer than ab-

---

[4]D. R. Corey and P. G. Schultz, "Generation of a Hybrid Sequence-Specific Single-Stranded Deoxyribonuclease," *Science* 238 (1987): 1401. Copyright 1987 by the AAAS. Reprinted by permission of publisher.

[5]Steven H. Young and Ida Chow, "Quantal Release of Transmitter Is Not Associated with Channel Opening on the Neuronal Membrane," *Science* 238 (1987): 1712. Copyright 1987 by the AAAS. Reprinted by permission of publisher.

stracts—sometimes several pages. A report may include
both an abstract and an executive summary.

Whether to use an abstract or an executive summary or both depends primarily on your audience and the purpose of your document. Many writers and readers become confused about the differences between an informative abstract and an executive summary (see preceding section).

Write an executive summary if:

- your readers are nontechnical

- your readers are more interested in your conclusions and recommendations than in your procedures

Write an abstract if:

- your readers have the same technical background as you do

- your readers are just as interested in your procedures and findings as in your conclusions and recommendations, or more so

Write both an abstract and an executive summary if you have a large audience with varied backgrounds and interests.

Because the executive summary is intended for those in management, emphasis should be placed on your project's big-picture implications for the organization. The summary stresses the purpose of your research and your conclusions and recommendations rather than your methods. Experts have presented various ratios for determining the appropriate length of a summary (for example, a 1-page summary for a 20-page report or a 1-page summary for a 50-page report), but only you can be the final judge of what key points must appear in your summary. Executive summaries do usually run longer than abstracts, and whereas abstracts rarely exceed 200 words, summaries sometimes run several pages.

Like abstracts (discussed in the preceding section), executive summaries should be informative and not merely descriptive of what the reader will find later in the report. Compare the following two summaries.

Noninformative Executive Summary:

The Hudson B Sand Unit is located in Harris County in southeastern Colorado. Searson International's working interest in the unit, covering 1900 gross acres, is 0.7565. The Hudson B sand reservoir has been producing since 19—, and the current unit well status is shown on the atttached map. This report represents the culmination of a study in which the profitability and potential of the Hudson B were investigated.

Many questions still remain: What is the current unit well status? What is the profitability and the potential of Hudson B?

Informative Executive Summary:

Our recent study of the Hudson B Sand Unit (located in Harris County in southeastern Colorado) reveals that current operating conditions and oil prices make the field uneconomical. The monthly operating loss is $3,056 and the net year-to-date loss is $26,044. (The net gain in 19— was $223,353.) Remaining reserves in the field are only 30,000 bbl, and average water cut is 92 percent. Current labor and transportation costs make tertiary recovery uneconomical, even if the current $16/bbl price doubles. We therefore recommend that Searson International sell the field.

Informative Executive Summary:

The Curtailment Statistical System (BT378) is designed to retain and report data for Universal's new Barbann Sales Division. The system will enhance present facilities and do much that is currently done manually. With this system, we estimate a savings of four work days per month in collecting operational data and preparing sales reports.

This new system design will:

- convert the user's curtailment file
- maintain the curtailment data through on-line inquiry and update utilities
- compute and store the database with the customers' daily allocations
- generate reports that compare supply levels with projected sales

The system will interface with the measurement system for daily and historical actual volumes and with the sales information system for key verification and customer/key-meter static information.

Data-Med recommends that the system be installed at all locations during the fourth quarter of 19—. We also recommend that principal users at each site run the system in a parallel/testing mode for the first three months.

The executive summary is not a promise; it does not just mention information that can only be found somewhere else in the report. Rather, the executive summary informs. If executives stop reading your report after its summary, will they be adequately informed about your work? If not, get more specific in your summary.

14.6   Body

Reports should be organized in a descending format, that is, from the big-picture message to supporting detail.

Almost all professors of English teach writers to begin their essays with once-upon-a-time details and then proceed to the and-they-lived-happily-ever-after final paragraphs. This format is appropriate for novelists like Stephen King and Agatha Christie; however, the ascending, chronological arrangement is probably the most serious flaw that occurs in technical report writing.

Readers do not understand details or the significance of details until they have the main message and a mental pegboard on which to hang those details as they read. Compare the ascending and descending arrangements presented in **Figure 14–2.** Always prefer a descending arrangement to give the reader the big-picture message that will be the basis for understanding and appropriating the rest of the report.

The Introduction

The introductory section should establish the writer's purpose and create a context for understanding the significant conclusions and recommendations.

Don't limit your thinking here to traditional background information. The "this is the problem and this is the way it has been done until now" approach is well worn and usually contains information that readers either already know or don't care to know. Unless your report will be important as an archival document, leave commonly known information out of your introduction.

Instead try a fresh approach. Begin with a statement of a problem, a striking quote, an apt analogy, a statement of universal need, a provocative question, or any other attention getter. Then lead into the purpose of the report and a definition of the project goal, explaining why the work was done at the present time or how it contributes to what has already been done on the subject. Also mention limitations of your report.

Provide only background that is essential to understanding conclusions. Much of the traditional background information included in reports fits best in the discussion section. And many of the "background" details should be omitted altogether.

Here is a suitable introduction to a report on a survey of Nevada crude oils:

> Minute quantities of volatile materials inherent in fossil fuels can adversely affect the quality of the environment when the fuels are consumed. Mercury (Hg) and selenium (Se) are two such materials. To determine whether Nevada crude oils contain these two elements, samples of crude from Nevada wells were subjected to neutron activation analysis.

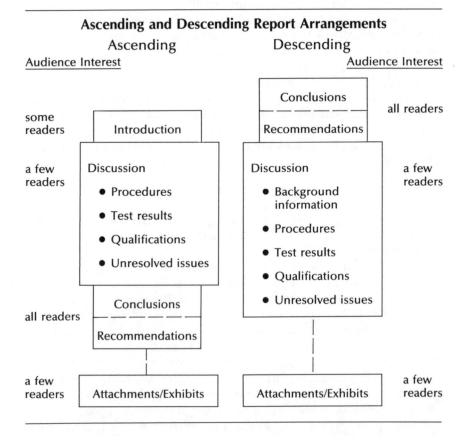

Figure 14–2. Ascending and descending report arrangements. Use the descending format for most reports.

Following are other introductions that immediately grab the reader's attention.

Analogy:

> The excitation of certain receptors in the brain can, it seems, be a two-edged sword. Although the receptors are part of the normal machinery for receiving incoming nerve signals, overstimulation of the receptors may damage, or even kill, the neurons on which they are located.[6]

Problem or Need:

> The 60 to 70 percent mortality rate associated with the adult respiratory distress syndrome (ARDS) has not improved since the syndrome was first described in 1967, despite improvements in supportive therapy.[7]

Startling Statement:

> Radar is losing its place as our primary protection against military attack.

Question:

> Oil and gas platforms in coastal waters pollute beaches every day of the year, right? Wrong. Seventy-five percent to 90 percent of the beach litter comes from offshore sources such as international shipping.
>
> • • •
>
> Should Belton International spend its limited funds on DO-CEL generators? Like all of life's big decisions, the answer depends on what we hope to accomplish by the transition. If . . .

Prediction:

> An exciting and completely unexpected perspective on the origin and distribution of cosmic-ray particles in the galaxy is coming from a series of ground-based observations that cover wavelengths in gamma-ray astronomy that are far beyond satellite capabilities. These extremely energetic gamma

---

[6]J. L. Marx, "Animals Yield Clues to Huntington's Disease," *Science* 238 (1987): 1510. Copyright 1987 by the AAAS. Reprinted by permission of publisher.

[7]Excerpted from material originally appearing in Gordon R. Bernard et al., "High-Dose Corticosteroids in Patients with the Adult Respiratory Distress Syndrome," *New England Journal of Medicine* 317 (1987): 1565. Reprinted by permission of publisher.

rays originate in the vicinity of neutron stars in binary systems. Although the processes by which they are produced
are yet poorly understood, nevertheless they have the potential to give us direct and detailed information about the
highest energy processes known in nature.[8]

The Conclusions

Although numbered statements are preferred, the conclusions may
be in paragraph form. Conclusions must always answer questions
raised by the stated purposes in the report. The conclusions, in other
words, present the results of the research findings.

In the conclusions, you should do the following:

- Summarize key facts or results
- Restate cautions or qualifications
- Mention alternative explanations or approaches
- Emphasize implications

Unless your reader will immediately understand the implications, you should avoid simply stating data or measurements. For
example:

> The temperature inside the controller box ranged from 46°
> to 62°C during the test.

This may be fine as a conclusion if your purpose was to determine
the temperature variations inside the controller. However, if your
purpose was to evaluate the accuracy of the controller under fluc-
tuating temperatures, then the following would be a much better
conclusion:

> The controller maintained a ±0.3 percent accuracy over a
> temperature range of 46°–62°C.

The Recommendations

The recommendation section takes the conclusions one step further
for the decision maker: You may recommend further areas of study,
the abandonment of research on a subject, changes in current policies
or procedures, or actions that management may take to capitalize on

---

[8]R. C. Lamb and T. C. Weekes, "Very High Energy Gamma-Ray Binary
Stars," *Science* 238 (1987): 1528. Copyright 1987 by the AAAS. Reprinted by
permission of publisher.

the research results—actions such as developing a new product or a new service.

The recommendation section is the most important section in many reports. It is here that you attempt to change human behavior—no small task. Unfortunately, many reports fail miserably in this section. Why? Because it's so easy to make high-sounding recommendations without addressing the problems involved in accomplishing them. For example, you conclude that overtorquing caused a component failure. Your recommendation is:

> Control the applied torque to within a range of 2500–2700 ft lb.

The recommendation, if followed, may solve the problem. But what if the available torque-measuring equipment is accurate only to ± 500 ft lb and new equipment is prohibitively expensive? If you ignore these facts, the recommendation becomes meaningless. It may get you off the hook with respect to the project, but your report does not ultimately change things for the better.

In short, make sure your report recommendations are doable.

The Discussion: Procedures, Test Results, Qualifications

The discussion section contains the supporting details for all that has gone before in the summary, conclusions, and recommendations. You may include:

- Experimental or preliminary research
- Descriptions of testing apparatus
- Testing procedures
- Testing or sampling errors and their significance
- Test results
- Interpretations of findings
- Explanations of alternative interpretations
- Qualifications
- Cautions

Keep in mind that few decision makers will read the discussion section in detail. So why write it, you may ask. For one thing, you need it to support your conclusions. For another, you need the details for the files and for later reference. Finally, secondary audiences will find the discussion details of interest.

Primarily, readers of this section will be other technical specialists interested in *how* and *why* you did what you did. They may build on your work, refute it, or further analyze or interpret it. But unless they are acting as secondary experts who are to advise management, they are reading primarily to be informed about your research, not to take managerial action.

The discussion is a necessary, but little-read, section of most reports.

Labeling the Document Sections

Forget the traditional generic titles of document sections mentioned here such as *Introduction, Conclusions, Recommendations,* and *Discussions.* Use other, more informative headings to help readers overview the contents and recall key ideas. (For a full discussion of headings, see **Section 10.7** on page 98.)

14.7   Appendix

The appendix contains supporting documentation (data presented in charts, tables, graphs, drawings, maps) that will be of interest only to a few secondary readers. A summary of the significant information from the tables or graphics should be included in the text of the report. A reader should not have to turn back and forth from text to appendix to read and understand the report.

Think of an appendix as one large footnote that is of interest mostly to secondary readers, not decision makers. Appendixes provide a way to present raw data and calculation methods to secondary readers without inundating your main audience, who has no interest in such detail. Never hide key information there without summarizing it in the text itself.

If primary readers need to see the information presented in an illustration or chart as they read your text, place the graphic in the text (not in the appendix) as near to the text reference as possible. Readers do not like to have to shuffle back and forth from text to appendix to read and understand the report itself. If you can summarize the data, put the summary in the text and the myriad other details in the appendix.

Number the appendixes in capital Roman numerals and title each one. Skimming readers will love you if you're accurate; they'll be infuriated if they run into a reference to Appendix D in the text and find no such attachment at the end of the report.

Because an appendix can go on forever, you can still appear to be a succinct, clear-thinking writer with a brief report containing only the significant details. But don't destroy that image by throwing into the appendix everything you learned in graduate school.

14.8 Glossary

A glossary lists in alphabetical order the symbols, abbreviations, and terms used in your report, along with their definitions.

A glossary provides definitions of terms or explanations of symbols and abbreviations used in the text of the report. It's virtually impossible for anyone to know all the standard symbols and abbreviations for every discipline. And even if that were possible, there is much duplication from one field of study to the next.

Therefore, analyze your audience to decide whether your report needs a glossary. Continually stopping to define or explain interrupts the flow of the report and becomes a nuisance to those readers with the same technical background as yours. But you have a responsibility to less-technical readers and those from other disciplines who may also make up your audience. You must provide them with the necessary definitions in a glossary, placed either at the beginning or at the end of the report.

Remember, too, that the benefit of a glossary is partially lost if its information is difficult to find; therefore, make sure entries are in alphabetical order.

15

Transmittal Documents

Transmittals for technical documents should accomplish at least one of four purposes: (1) provide an executive overview of the report, proposal, or contract, (2) make comments you don't want to include in the primary document, (3) answer questions you anticipate from your reader's review of the report or proposal, (4) call for a decision or action.

In the old days when corporate chains of command really meant something, transmittal letters were stacked one on top of another like silt layers in a sedimentary basin. Beginning with the report's originator, through office, district, region, division, and headquarters, the ubiquitous transmittals multiplied layer upon layer. (In fact, recent archaeological evidence suggests that originally cardboard was formed by the fossilization of transmittal letters.) Their chief value was to suggest that each lower-level manager in the chain had actually read the report. This allowed the higher-level managers to transmit the report upward *without* bothering to read it themselves. Think about it.

Far too many routine transmittals attached to reports and proposals find their way around an organization only to clutter desks and reading files. If you are sending the same transmittal document that your subordinate sent you (changing only the date, name, and report title), you can probably eliminate the transmittal altogether because no doubt it's too generic to be useful.

If you're sending a transmittal only to have a record of the submission of the report or proposal—the names and date of submission—that information can be included on the title page of the primary document itself.

Write a transmittal only for the following purposes:

- To explain why you are submitting the document ("in response to RFP #8883" or "in response to Vice President Harry Sloan's request for documentation of final testing procedures . . .")

- To overview for senior executives the primary features, benefits, or conclusions of your report or proposal

- To emphasize any special points, such as a deadline for decisions, volume discount, special offer, or effective date of bid

- To explain anything unusual, such as an omission, exception, caution, or change

- To ask for a decision or any other follow-up action

Compare the following two versions of a transmittal accompanying a proposal to a client. Note how the changes make the difference between an effective transmittal and one that leaves confusion.

Transmittal (Version 1)

Dear Mr. Harrison:

Enclosed for execution by your company are three copies each of the following documents:

- RHP Form 994, page 6 (proposal page)
- RHP Form 994C, page 13 (contractor's bond)
- RHP Form 334, listing of all maps

These documents are necessary for executing the contract between your company and ours for the purchase, delivery, and installation of subscriber carrier equipment.

Upon execution of the enclosed documents, please return them to our office.

Sincerely,

Problems with and questions about this routine transmittal were numerous in the company that originated this letter: (1) Readers didn't send back all three copies of the required documents. (2) The appropriate signatures were not on the documents. (3) The recipients didn't select a reputable bonding agency. (4) The recipients called the writer with questions that only the project engineers could correctly answer.

— Because of these problems and questions and the ensuing desperation of the readers "to get it right," the transmittal was finally rewritten in accordance with the preceding guidelines. As a result, the letter became much more effective in accomplishing its purpose. (The improvements are printed in boldface.)

Transmittal (Version 2)

Dear Mr. Harrison:

Enclosed for execution by your company are three copies each of the following documents necessary for executing the contract between your company and ours for the purchase, delivery, and installation of subscriber carrier equipment:

- RHP Form 994, page 6 (proposal page)

- RHP Form 994C, page 13 (contractor's bond)
- RHP Form 334, listing of all maps

Please note that all three copies of these documents must be signed by either the president or a vice president of your company.

Additionally, the bond (RHP Form 994C) must be furnished by a surety or sureties listed by the United States Treasury Department as acceptable.

Upon execution of the enclosed documents, please return them to our office. **Because we handle only the processing of these contracts, if you have specific questions about the contracts or maps themselves, we suggest that you contact engineer Bill Jones directly at 234-5678.**

Sincerely,

In summary then, transmittals for technical documents should accomplish at least one of four purposes:

1. Provide an executive overview
2. Make comments you don't want to include in the primary report or proposal
3. Answer questions anticipated after your reader's review of the report or proposal
4. Call for a decision or action

Figure 15–1 contains an example of a transmittal letter of the kind that accompanies a proposal.

Transmittal Letter

Dear Mr. Garcia:

We submit the accompanying proposal plan for a high- and low-voltage monitor to use on a single-phase 120v electrical outlet. After thoroughly studying the project, we think our proposed design offers both a practical and marketable monitor. Simplicity will be the key to user acceptance of this product.

The accompanying preliminary schedule of the work provides ample time to complete the various tasks by May 1, and we are confident that we can adhere to this schedule despite the possible delays you mentioned in our initial meeting.

Project engineer Richard Adams will call you on August 16 to see if you are ready for us to begin this project. We're looking forward to designing this attractive new product for you.

Sincerely,

Figure 15–1. Transmittal letter. Transmittals should say more than "Here it is."

16

Status Reports

Status reports should link past and present work to the future. These reports have two main purposes: to keep management informed about your work and to aid in your own final report preparation. Status reports do not necessarily have to present positive results or give final conclusions.

A status report describes the progress being made on research, on a design, or on a manufacturing process. Progress is measured against predetermined project objectives, specifications, schedules, and budgets.

Why prepare status reports? Some researchers dread the preparation of such reports because they consider them an unnecessary nuisance. (And some are, particularly when requests come too frequently.) But to lessen the irritation, consider status reports as *part of your work* rather than an interruption of it. And remember that management has invested stockholder resources in your project and is, therefore, duty-bound to keep track of it.

The primary purpose of status reports is to keep management informed—to report on budgets and schedules that may need to be adjusted or to report trends that may be cause for changing the direction of your work or abandoning the project altogether. But a secondary benefit, one of the chief benefits to you as the writer, is that these periodic reports will help you in completing the final project report. Not incidently, regular informative status reports will make your bosses' jobs easier, will make them look better, and will endear you to them at performance review time.

These reports seem particularly difficult for writers involved in long, ongoing projects, because they often feel that (1) they haven't accomplished "enough" to report, (2) they have only negative results to report, or (3) their reports are repetitious.

What Is Progress?

Writers should keep in mind that these reports are simply steps to a final project outcome. Therefore, progress does not necessarily mean *completion* of any one phase. Consider preparatory work as progress: development of sampling or testing procedures, the ordering of equipment, or negotiations with suppliers.

There's even progress in failure. When you run into a blind alley, say so. When you have tentative results or conclusions, say so. All these interim phases, obstacles, or problems are part of moving toward the final results, conclusions, and recommendations.

Also remember that some repetition is inevitable and even desirable in status reports. That is, most management readers need a reminder of the purpose of your work and what had happened the last time you reported. Your periodic report should *briefly* bring them up to date on the why and what of your past work, focus on the present interim period, and then *briefly* project future work (see **Figure 16–1**).

Management will usually have these key questions in mind when reading your status report:

- Are you ahead of, behind, or on schedule?

- Are you ahead of, behind, or on target with cost projections?

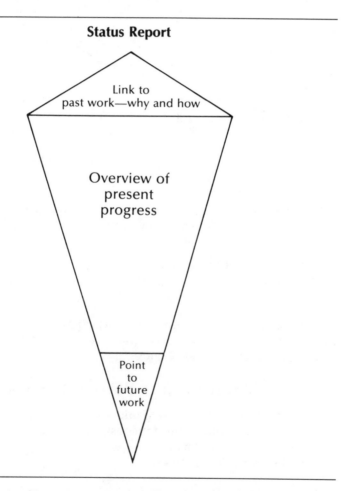

Status Report

Link to past work—why and how

Overview of present progress

Point to future work

Figure 16–1. Status report. Status reports link past, present, and future, but primarily focus on the present.

Graphic Presentation of a Status Report
MONTHLY PROJECT COST
June 19--

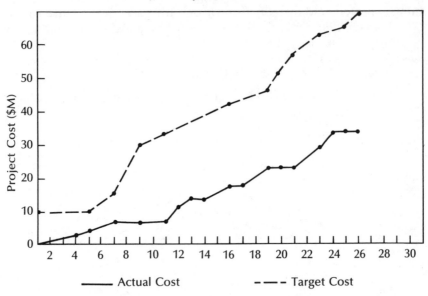

Figure 16–2. Graphic presentation of a status report. An effective status report graph shows time relationships and compares actual figures with projections.

- Have you discovered anything that will materially change the objectives, course, cost, or chance of success of the project? If so, what is it and what are its effects?

Keep in mind that nothing beats a graphic presentation for showing progress toward goals over time—two of the three primary concerns of management (see **Figure 16–2**).

Multiproject Status Reports

One special difficulty in organizing status reports is finding an appropriate format when simultaneously reporting on several ongoing projects. When such reporting is required, we suggest the multiproject format shown in **Figure 16–3**.

Format for Multiproject Status Reports

EXECUTIVE SUMMARY
(Use informative subheads and/or bullets to give a one- or two-sentence overview of progress and major recommendations, if any, for each project.)

PROJECT #1 MAJOR HEADING
Link to Past
Present Status
Next Step
(These sections are expansions of the brief overview given in the executive summary. All points may be covered in a single paragraph.)

PROJECT #2 MAJOR HEADING
Link to Past
Present Status
Next Step

PROJECT #3 MAJOR HEADING
Link to Past
Present Status
Next step

ATTACHMENTS
(Data sheets for optional reading.)

Figure 16–3. Format for multiproject status reports. This special status report format allows readers to skim quickly for highlights regarding several projects.

17

Service and Inspection Reports

A service and inspection report may focus on an activity, a failure, a malfunction, or an accident and its cause. The condition of the equipment, site, or system after the reported activity or problem is always a consideration. Finally, recommendations about preventive maintenance and other issues are of major interest to decision makers.

The biggest temptation (and flaw) in writing service and inspection reports is to begin at the beginning and present the details in chronological order. Writers err, too, in telling the reader all about the trouble involved in performing the test or putting the system, equipment, or site back in operation.

Begin your report with a summary statement of what happened, what the results were, and why. Then follow up with recommendations and supporting details and data (see **Figure 17–1.**)

The primary task, however, in such a report is to analyze the reasons for any problem or deficiency. If the causes cannot be determined, say so directly; don't avoid addressing this issue.

Include your opinion on whether this is a one-time, infrequent, or recurring problem, as well as any relevant facts. Such information will possibly suggest more-expensive preventive maintenance, replacement of equipment, or revised operating procedures or service.

Finally, calculate, if appropriate, any time and dollar loss due to the failure so that management can assess alternatives for prevention.

Service and Inspection Report

To:

From:

Subject:

The top bearing combination on the Spindle Bottom 600 failed for the second time in a month. The motor was supplied with a top bearing combination of 9320 UPDT/7320 PDT with a 40° angle of contact. This bearing combination is designed for large downthrust loads, and it is receiving only about half its design load. Therefore, the inner ring of the bearing in contact with the shaft tends to slide across the ball bearings instead of rotating them. This condition causes extreme heat buildup and premature bearing failure.

WRC has two available options; I recommend option 1.

1. Reduce the contact angle to 29° to allow more downthrust bearing contact.

2. Remove the balls from the 7320 bearing. This action will put the total downward thrust on the 9320 bearing and cause the balls in this bearing to rotate.

WRC normally does not stock bearings with a 29° angle, and there is a 28-week wait on delivery. If you decide to approve option one, we need to order as soon as possible to keep downtime to the minimum. Total cost will be approximately $1200 for option 1 or $400 for option 2.

The attached drawing illustrates both modifications with the proper 29° angle.

Figure 17–1. Service and inspection report. Inspection reports should focus on what happened, what were the results, and why. Recommendations and supporting details should follow.

18

Specifications

> *Specifications should include an overview of the project, product, or service. This overview gives an obvious framework for the detailed contractual obligation that may also include drawings and conditions of the contract. The text and drawings should complement each other, not compete. Avoid loophole words and vague generalizations.*

Specifications usually accompany the purchase of technical products or services. Their purpose is to protect both the buyer and the seller by clearly outlining the requirements both parties are expected to meet.

The buyer's obligation is usually fairly well understood—pay for the product in a certain currency by a certain time. Thus, most of the specifications will focus on the seller's obligation. Most specifications will be written by (or on behalf of) buyers, who may take either of two approaches: the method approach or the results approach.

The *method approach* details specifically what materials, products, designs, or services should be used and in what way they should be used. Specifications following the method approach have three main parts:

1. Scope, assumptions, and general conditions under which the work is to be performed
2. Description of materials, equipment, fixtures, and the manufacturing process used in the development and production of the product or service
3. Specific details concerning workmanship, installation, operation, and application

The *results approach* specifies the results and leaves the contractor to choose the methods and materials.

Acceptance Testing

Whether the method or results approach is used, the seller's obligations are usually spelled out in terms of tests that must be passed. These tests may begin with qualification of raw material, may include intermediate manufacturing steps, and usually will include functional testing of the final product.

Remember, every test outlined in the specifications must include four distinct steps:

1. Establishing the acceptance criteria

2. Selecting the test methods
3. Outlining the test procedure
4. Deciding what to do with material that fails

Omitting one of these steps will open doors to future disagreement and substandard products. For example, consider the following, taken from specifications for high-pressure gate valves:

> Valves shall pass a 30-minute gas test at 10,000 psi without leakage.

While this seems straightforward enough, several potential loopholes become apparent upon a step-by-step examination:

- The acceptance criterion is that there are "no leaks." But what is a leak?
- As for the test method, what kind of gas is to be used? Air? Helium? Is the valve to be submerged in water to detect leaks?
- The test procedure includes a 30-minute hold time, but what else is required? A pressure recorder? A witness? Tests to hold pressure in both directions? Tests with the gate fully open?
- What if a valve fails? Are retests permitted? Are repairs permitted?

The following test specifications close these loopholes:

> Each valve shall be nitrogen-tested to 10,000 psi from both upstream and downstream sides against the closed gate. In addition, the valve body shall be nitrogen-tested to 10,000 psi with the gate fully open and both ends flanged. All tests shall continue for 30 minutes after 10,000 psi has been reached. Strip-chart recorders shall be used to document time at pressure. The valve shall be submerged in clear water during testing for visual detection of leaks. No leaks are permitted. A leak is defined as a nitrogen flow greater than five bubbles per minute from any part of the valve or test fixture. Any valve leaking around the end flanges, gate, or stem packing may be repaired and retested. However, no repair welding is allowed on any part of the valve or valve bonnet. Any valve leaking through the body shall be scrapped.

Accompanying Drawings

Information contained in drawings that accompany specifications should not overlap information contained in the text. Such overlapping may result in contradictions and confusion. If you must repeat information in both the text and the drawings, make sure the wording is identical in both places. Drawings should include:

- Site of materials, equipment, fixtures, or service
- Overall dimensions and sizes
- Interworking of materials, equipment, or service

Finally, specifications require that attention be given to wording choices such as the following.

Shall Versus *Will*

Use the imperative *shall* rather than *will* in describing the work that must be done. When establishing a term or condition, however, use the indicative verb *is*:

> A forging or wrought product is [*not* shall be] unacceptable if the signal loss is greater than 50 percent of the reference back reflection.

"All the Rest"

When describing kinds or grades of materials, start with the exceptional situations. For these, specify size, quality or location, and then lump all the other materials into an exceptions paragraph: "All the rest shall be. . . ."

Numerals

Use numerals rather than spelled out numbers.

Imperatives

The passive voice (defined and illustrated more fully in **Section 12.3**) leaves the doer of the action out of a sentence. The result is often confusion about who is responsible for what in a particular process. For example:

> The lines should be flushed with boiling water for 12 hours. (Who is to do this? The installer? The client upon first use?)

To be clear in distinguishing responsibility, use the imperative:

Flush the lines with boiling water for 12 hours before start-up.

You will also be clear if you use the active voice and third person:

The installer should flush the lines with boiling water for 12 hours before start-up.

"One or More" Phrases

Specifications frequently refer to rejections with the "one or more" phrase. However, if one flaw is reason enough for rejecting the part, equipment, material, or process, then "or more" is redundant.

A forging or wrought product is unacceptable if the height of any indication exceeds reference level. (It would be redundant to write "one or more indications.")

Either/Or

Use *either/or* only when you are stating a choice:

Fill the ditches with either mulch or sand.

And/Or

Avoid the use of *and/or*; instead use either *both* or *or*. If your intention is to emphasize that the combination of both is not meant, use *and not both*.

Not:

Cold laps and/or quench cracks are defects.

But:

Both cold laps and quench cracks are defects.

Et Cetera

Use *et cetera* (etc.) only when its meaning can be correctly inferred from the objects, data, or events explicitly listed.

Not:

Fill the ditches with mulch, etc. (What's the et cetera? Old golf balls? Manure? Mesquite?)

Correct use:

> The poles should be interlocked in the following manner:
> 1 to 3, 2 to 4, 3 to 5, 4 to 6, etc.

Articles

Spec writers often make their writing sound clipped by omitting articles such as *a*, *an*, and *the*. Although their omission makes sentences more concise, clarity often is a problem. Without the articles in the following sentence, a reader could misread "blank off ends" and "connections to test medium" as adjective-noun combinations rather than actions. ("Blank-off ends" is an adjective-noun combination; "to blank off the ends" is an action. "Connections-to-test medium" is an adjective-noun combination; "connections to test the medium" tells the purpose of the connections.)

> Blank off (the) ends of (the) valve and make necessary connections to test (the) medium.

To avoid misreading and make your writing flow smoothly, keep the articles in your writing.

Misplaced Modifiers

Make sure descriptive or qualifying words, phrases, and clauses come as close to the words they describe as possible.

Confusing:

> All leak testing of flanged components shall be performed with the correct metal-seal-ring gasket for sealing **prior to the addition of body-filler grease.**

Clear:

> Prior to the addition of body filler grease, all leak testing of flanged components shall be performed by use of the correct metal-seal-ring gasket.

Confusing:

> Measurements shall be taken on all critical components **after the final heat treatment.**

Clear:

> After final heat treatment of components, measurements shall be taken on all the critical ones.

Confusing:

> Packing for the upper and lower stems on all valves must be installed with the use of a special fixture **witnessed by Arabomo, Inc.**

Clear:

> Arabomo, Inc. must witness the installation of packing for the upper and lower stems on all valves. This installation requires the use of a special fixture.

Vague Generalities

Avoid vague generalities that will require a lawsuit to enforce or defend:

> Designed to the satisfaction of the project engineer . . .
>
> Acceptable to the client . . .
>
> Chemical impurities may be cause for rejection.
>
> Testing procedures may be waived at the discretion of the inspector.
>
> Additional trips to the site may be required.
>
> Aerial photos may be required.

19

Procedures and Operating Instructions

> *Begin all procedures and operating instructions with an overview statement about the task. Use an appropriate instruction format and page layout to aid the reader in following the procedure. Place safety precautions before the step in which they should be taken. Separate action steps from explanations. Number steps. Put each action in a separate sentence. Link ideas clearly. Use the active voice. Avoid backward "Then . . . if" statements. Avoid loops and go-to directions even if you must be repetitious. Use illustrations liberally. Test your instructions.*

1. **Begin all procedures and operating instructions with an overview statement about the task.**

Example: This procedure will convert numeric values to string values. This function differs from STR$ because it does not really change the bytes of the data—just the way BASIC interprets those bytes.

2. **Use an appropriate instructional format and page layout to guide the reader quickly from step to step.**

Explanation: If you follow the guidelines in this chapter, you will have designed a functional format. The reader should be able to skim, quickly separating actions from explanations and examples. Use bold print, italics, various typefaces, headings, indentation, and adequate white space to guide the reader's eye.

3. **Place safety precautions *before* the step in which they should be taken.**

Example: CAUTION: Prior to performing any tests on a point-to-point or multipoint private line, have a transmission circuit layout (TCL) card available. This card will allow you to identify the 4-wire facility before proceeding to the next step.

4. **Separate action steps from explanations.**

Example: Close all open files. Delete all variables and program lines currently residing in memory before you load the specified program. If you omit the R option, BALCO should return to direct mode.

Explanation: In the preceding sentence, where does the action stop and the explanation start? It's difficult to tell. In contrast, notice how easy it is to distinguish each step from each example or explanation throughout this chapter.

5. Number all steps. Use bullets or indentations for all explanations.

Explanation: Numbers suggest a chronological order to a procedure. To number explanations, examples, or any other items confuses readers about whether some order is involved. Therefore, reserve numbers for sequences of actions. Use bullets or indentations for subpoints in explanations that do not involve sequences of actions.

6. Describe each action in a separate sentence.

Example: Insert the data disk in Drive A. Insert the utility disk in Drive B.

7. Link ideas clearly.

Example (unclear): Set the transmit amplifier control to the full counterclockwise position and deactivate the detector. (Are these two separate actions? Do you do them simultaneously? Is this a cause-and-effect relationship?)

Example (clear): Set the transmit amplifier control to the full counterclockwise position *as* you deactivate the detector.

Example (clear): Set the transmit amplifier control to the full counterclockwise position, *thus* deactivating the detector.

Example (clear): Set the transmit amplifier control to the full counterclockwise position. *Then* deactivate the detector.

8. Use the active voice.

Example (passive voice): The scan lines are numbered beginning with 0 at the top of the character position by the F2 command.

Example (active voice): The F2 command numbers the scan lines beginning with 0 at the top of the character position.

Example (active voice): Use the F2 command to number the

scan lines beginning with 0 at the top of the character position.

9. Avoid backward "Then . . . if" statements.

Example (backward statement): Press RETURN to continue printing if the KP message appears.

Example (improved): If the KP message appears, press RETURN to continue printing.

10. Avoid loops and go-to directions even if you must be repetitious.

Explanation: Readers do not like to be given the runaround with procedures any more than callers or visitors to your office. Don't refer them back and forth from section to section to find steps or explanations that appear elsewhere ("Turn to section XX and proceed as directed there"). Procedure writers sometimes fear being repetitious and wasting space by repeating directions. However, wasted user time and errors resulting from confusion are far more expensive than duplicated information.

11. Use illustrations liberally.

12. Test your instructions.

Explanation: Have someone with little or no knowledge of the task or equipment work through the procedure. If he or she has difficulty, revise the instructions. Do not assume that the real end user will have a better technical background and understanding than your "man on the street."

20

Proposals for External Readers

20.1   The Proposal as a Sales Tool

To be used as a sales tool, a proposal must incorporate a strategy, address the reader's needs, and then persuasively present the proposer's solution and capabilities.

"We write proposals but we don't want them to *look* like proposals— we want them to sound like informational, technical reports," a client told us. Although we didn't go into a philosophical discussion with him, we filed the remark away as a basic misconception about proposals.

Selling an idea or solution needn't be akin to selling used cars on local TV. Nevertheless, a proposal must be attractive. It must be everything a good sales letter is—but much more specific. A proposal presents a problem or need and persuasively outlines a project, service, or product that the proposer can oversee or provide to solve the problem or meet the need.

You may find yourself offering a proposal in one of two situations. (1) You send an unsolicited proposal to persuade the reader he or she needs a product or service. (2) The reader is aware of a need, but you must persuade him or her that you are the best source for the product or service that will meet the need.

Your proposal may, in fact, take the form of a single-page sales letter, a formal two-thousand-page document, or a sheet with only price quotations and specifications.

It's usually not the form of a proposal but its substance that brings rejection. However, a sloppy proposal does leave a lasting negative impression about the quality of your service or product. Therefore, avoid the following common proposal weaknesses.

No Strategy

The most important feature of your proposal should be your theme or strategy, which is repeated and developed throughout the document. Why should the bidder select *your* organization over all the rest? Do you have the best design? Do you have the most thoroughly trained technicians? Do you have the most up-to-date equipment or information? Can you do the project most inexpensively? Can you do it more quickly than the competition? Give your reader one or two basic overriding themes to capsule your capabilities. Avoid saying simply, "Well, so can we!"

Carelessness about
Apples-to-Oranges Comparisons

Help your reader remember the key points when comparing your offer to the offers of your competitors. Clearly identify the important issues and then point out how you can address each. Force the reader to evaluate the competition with regard to *your* issues.

Failure to Show Adequate
Understanding of the Problem

Some proposers have all the answers before they hear the questions. A necessary part of your job is to communicate to the reader a full understanding of the problem or objective so that he or she will be convinced your solution is the appropriate one.

Answers to the Wrong Problems

Study the client's request for proposal (RFP). Propose to do what the prospective buyer wants. Notice that we didn't say you should necessarily propose to do what the buyer *says* he or she wants—make sure you investigate those stated needs or wants. What an RFP says and what can be gleaned from a discussion with the buyer may be vastly different.

Many, including us, have learned this truth the hard way. A few years back, we received a request to propose a training program, a request that already included within it a detailed seminar outline. Because there were several places where we considered improvements could be made to the seminar outline, we called the prospective client and asked if the topics were firmly set. "Oh, yes. That's exactly what we want. All our VP's and technical experts have signed off on that topic outline."

Therefore, we developed our proposal along those lines, only to have the proposal rejected. The client's explanation: "The winning proposer completely scrapped our seminar outline. What her company presented makes a lot more sense, and we're really excited about her changes."

You perhaps will discover the differences between stated needs and criteria and the real needs only by flushing out and investigating discrepancies. Give clients what they need, but be sure to find out what the *real* needs are. Trying to discover the real needs is especially important if you are providing products or services that the prospective client may not understand as fully as you do.

Vagueness

Proposers often fear that they will give away too much information in outlining their approaches and solutions to problems. There is, of course, always the danger of having a prospective buyer read your proposal and attempt to implement your solution without your help. But the bigger fear should be of giving so little detail that the reader doesn't think you know how to do the job.

One often vague section in proposals is the list of references. Name contacts and provide addresses and phone numbers.

Closely related to vagueness about references is evasiveness about the background and experience of the proposed project staff: "have graduate degrees in related areas," "has had ten years' experience in the industry," "has handled similar projects both nationally and internationally." Readers often interpret such comments thus: "Nothing to brag about, huh?"

Extravagant Claims

Readers raise eyebrows when organizations claim to have expertise in everything but the treatment of ingrown toenails of rabbits. Be wary of hyperbolic language—phrases such as "the most extensive," "the most authoritative," "unequaled," "the undisputed leader." Tone claims down to the point at which you can support them with facts. Instead of high-flown language, include published articles, survey results, test data, testimonial letters, or sample products—whatever supports your claims. Overstatement begs your reader to be skeptical.

Failure to Provide Memory Aids

By the time a buyer reviews five or six lengthy proposals, disorientation sets in. Which proposer claims to be able to do what, why, where, when, how, and at what cost? Don't assume that your reader will be as eager to work at understanding and remembering your key points as you are. Instead, provide help by way of overview statements in each section, summary blurbs beside lengthy text, informative headings, and high-impact graphics with full captions.

20.2   Nine Parts of a Formal Proposal

A proposal must (1) analyze the buyer's need or problem, (2) present the technical solution to the problem, (3) discuss the management and business issues, and (4) persuade the buyer that the proposer is the best suited to do the work. A formal proposal can accomplish these objectives with a variety of organizational formats and informative headings.

There are at least as many ways to organize a proposal as there are industries. Your specific project will determine, for example, if you need a section entitled "Deliverables" or "Testing Procedures." Most proposals, however, should follow the general structure of a formal report, with an executive overview and the remainder of the document in descending format (see **Section 14.6**).

But whatever arrangement and specific divisions you select, a proposal should

- present a thorough analysis of the buyer's needs or problems
- propose technical solutions
- discuss the management and business considerations of the project
- persuade the buyer that the proposer is the best suited to do the work.

The following describes nine parts that should be included in most proposals:

Title Page

The title page should contain the following:

- A title indicative of what you are proposing
- The name of the recipient
- The date of submission
- Any RFP, contract, or project number
- Any statement of security or confidentiality

Table of Contents

For proposals of more than 10–12 pages, there should be a table of contents that lists informative subheads so as to provide another review of benefits and other key issues.

List of Exhibits

The exhibits should have informative titles (for example, not "Cost Analysis" but "Cost Comparison of Video and Software Production").

Matrix Response Sheet

The matrix response sheet is a two-column chart listing the stated evaluation criteria and the pages that respond to each point.

Executive Summary

An executive summary should state the following:

- Who you are
- What the problem is
- How you propose to solve the problem
- What the key benefits will be
- How you'll manage and evaluate the project
- How long you will take to complete the project
- How much the project will cost (unless costs are required in a separate document)

Analysis of the Problem, Need, or Situation

This analysis should include the following:

- A discussion of the proposal problem, mission, and goals *in terms of results*
- The specifications established by the buyer
- The assumptions and qualifications imposed on the research
- A literature search of past work done
- Client-provided data as support
- The proposed solution
- The advantages of the solution
- The feasibility of the solution
- A plan for performance testing and measurement of the solution
- Alternative solutions and pros and cons of each

Approach to the Solution or Proposed Project

This part of the proposal should include the following:

- Plans for various phases, experiments, and tasks (a flowchart is helpful here)
- Management and staff requirements

- A description of equipment and site preparation
- Contingency plans
- Scheduling and procedures
- Deliverables (quantitative and qualitative data)
- Control and quality assurance plans
- Evaluations
- Certifications
- A schedule of meetings with the buyer
- Progress reports and final reports
- Costs, methods, and terms of payment
- Guarantees

Credentials

The credentials provided should include:

- Those of the proposing organization (specific company references, with names, addresses, and phone numbers of contact persons; past achievements and awards; facilities; equipment; personnel)
- Those of the assigned staff (patents, achievements, awards, publications; years of experience in what positions with what companies; involvement in relevant projects; education)

Miscellaneous Exhibits

Among such exhibits might be:

- Brochures
- Testimonials
- Certifications
- Patents
- Published articles
- A list of similar jobs completed (with references) and other evidence

21

Manuals

21.1   Objectives for Developing a Manual

Manuals must be accessible, readable, motivational, and maintainable. Far too many manuals sit unread on organizational shelves because they're poorly designed. Readers demand functional manuals that allow them to get a task done quickly without a big investment of learning time.

Just a few years ago, the only people who read computer manuals were technical professionals, who weren't afraid of them. Nowadays, everybody has a use for them. And these readers are becoming more and more discerning about the documentation and other operational manuals they must plow through to get their jobs done. There is an old joke that users could evaluate a software package's documentation by first checking the bookstore to see how many books had been written to interpret the manufacturer's standard documentation.

The joke is no longer funny. Users want to be productive immediately, and if they can't learn how to complete a specific task quickly and easily, they tend to skip the directions altogether and work by trial and error.

Therefore, if manuals of any kind are to serve a useful purpose— other than job security for the manual designer— they must meet the following criteria.

Accessibility

The key decisions in designing a manual revolve around the answer to this question: Who will use the manual and for what purpose?

Novices need instructional manuals—tutorials and demonstrations—that give step-by-step procedures and explanations for accomplishing specific tasks.

Experienced users need only a reference book containing key definitions, facts, and codes so they can look up terms and procedures (in condensed form) that they may have never needed before or may have learned but forgotten.

To be functional and accessible, an instructional manual should not be combined with a reference manual. In cases where the two are combined, beginners become confused and discouraged because so much vital information is "left out," and experienced users become impatient with the "unnecessary" detail and explanation included in the tutorials.

Also important for accessibility are brevity and simplicity. Readers don't want to wade through unnecessary information to find what they need for completing a task. And when they find their subject, they want to understand it. Therefore, the primary focus of manuals should be on how to's and benefits, with only brief mention (if any) of specifications and short explanations about how things work.

Finally, information becomes more accessible with informative tables of contents, indexes, headings, and page or section titles (for example, not "File Names," but "Changing a File Name" or "Creating a File Name").

Accessibility permits readers to have control in searching for what they need to know. Keep in mind that few manuals will be read cover to cover.

Readability

To make manuals readable, follow these guidelines:

- Break concepts into small units and tasks.
- Allow adequate white space.
- Provide informative headings.
- Provide overview statements of objectives.
- Give frequent illustrations and examples.
- Use short sentences and simple words.
- Keep one major idea to a sentence.
- Take the "you" approach and use imperatives for actions the reader must perform.

As an example of how to simplify your sentences, consider the following.

Complex:

> In addition to the headings already produced during first-page processing, the one-line representation of the code-block sequence associated with the subledger number should be printed because this enhancement is aimed at the readability of the fiche output.

Simple

> To make the fiche output more readable, print the first-page processing and the one-line representation of the code-block sequence of the subledger number.

Using imperatives results in directions that are clear and forceful.

Don't Write:

> If this test is to be used with damaged equipment, reference should be made to the CD/SD for the determination of the extent of the necessary modifications.

But:

> If you are testing damaged equipment, refer to the CD/SD to determine the necessary changes.

Don't Write:

> The display signal cable should be disconnected from the expansion unit.

But:

> Disconnect the signal cable from the expansion unit.

Motivational

To motivate readers to do something, learn something, or operate something they fear or are reluctant to try, most manuals must be motivational. They must make the tasks seem simple and worthwhile. Meeting the first two criteria mentioned—accessibility and readability—will go far toward achieving this goal.

Additionally, manual writers should turn features into benefits.

Not Features:

> You can sort your information alphabetically or numerically.

> You can append your files.

But Benefits:

> You can locate and sort customer files by date of contact or last order, by geographic region, or by products frequently ordered.

> You can join short chapters or segments of your reports into one file of any length.

Ease of Updating

Manuals start becoming obsolete before the ink dries. Therefore, a major consideration, often overlooked, is the need to provide a document that can be easily updated. When readers refer to a manual repeatedly only to find outdated information, they soon stop using it altogether. To be functional, then, manuals must be designed so that they can accommodate added or revised pages or new subjects and sections.

Give considerable attention to manual updating before you go to press with your first edition.

21.2   Six Phases of Developing a Manual

Developing a manual involves six key phases: planning, storyboarding, preparing visuals, drafting, revising, updating. Shortchanging any phase will result in a seriously flawed manual.

Writers of manuals tend to err in one of three ways. (1) They don't plan the project at all. (2) They design and organize the manual for the wrong audience. (3) They don't draft and edit the text effectively.

Planning

When assigned a major task such as developing a manual, some people, in their attempt to get the project under way, begin to draft the text immediately—just to get something on paper with which to work. That is an effective method of drafting text—as fast as possible in as few sittings as possible. But the drafting stage must be preceded by intensive planning. Otherwise, the drafting will result in little more than reams of paper containing useless sentences that have to be moved, patched, recast, or deleted altogether.

In fact, in our own experience, we've found that fully 50 percent of any writing effort involves planning the design and collecting the necessary background data and information. If you're going to allow yourself three months to write a manual, six weeks of that time should be spent in:

- determining who your audience will be
- interviewing members of your audience or observing what they need to know to do their job
- determining what they already know about the subject
- learning what basic content to include.

(The preceding section details how this audience analysis results in a decision as to whether to prepare a reference manual, an instructional manual, or a motivational manual.)

Only after a thorough audience analysis and decisions about what your readers need are you ready to lay out your manual.

Storyboarding

The rule that should guide a technical writer with a message to communicate is this: Show, don't tell. That is the single most important principle in manual design. People prefer to be shown how to do a task rather than to be told. Therefore, the more visual your manual is, the better.

Don't think of your writing project in terms of paragraphs and concepts to be explained. Think of it as a manual for skimmers—with a few words, headlines, bulleted lists, and graphics to catch the eye and draw attention to important information.

To achieve this effect, visualize the entire manual before you begin to write any of the text. The technical term for this visualization is *storyboarding*. The general framework for all manuals includes front matter, the main text, and the appendixes.

Within this general framework, you first lay out the manual in skeleton form, only adding the "meat" much later. The skeleton will contain titles of the concepts to be included, a brief overview of the key concepts to be explained, bulleted subordinate points, mention of analogies or explanations to be used, and graphic illustrations. The brief overviews, of two or three sentences each, force you to organize your thoughts and provide a reminder to you of what goes in each section.

Different writers find that different storyboarding techniques work for them. Here are a few of the most common.

Flipchart Method.   Hang flipchart pages around the room and then walk around to review and revise their order. When you have them in the most logical order, draft the text by developing the sketchy ideas on each flipchart sheet. (See **Figures 21–1** and **21–2** for an illustration of this method.)

Index Card Method.   Use 4″ × 6″ index cards to plan each concept. On a large countertop or desk, arrange the cards into a logical sequence. Then draft the full text from the ideas on the cards.

Colored Paper Method.   Use 8½″ × 11″ sheets of variously colored paper to plan the concepts. For example, use blue sheets for the background board for each concept. Print headings on each page with a black felt-tip pen. Lay red rectangles on the blue pages to represent graphics. Place yellow rectangles on the blue pages to represent workbook exercises. Drop pink rectangles on the blue pages to signify

Storyboarding for a Training Manual

Sheet 1

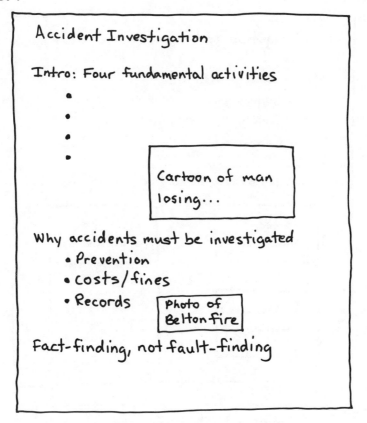

(continued on next page)

Figure 21–1. Storyboarding for a training manual. A storyboard plan for a training manual contains only the skeleton of ideas.

photos of equipment. Green rectangles might mean that the operator will be instructed to turn on the video player for a demonstration of the concept.

Edmond H. Weiss in his book *How to Write a Usable User Manual* does an excellent job of applying his own principles for computer manuals. His model was developed by Hughes Aircraft Corporation many years ago:

1. The control bar—document section and page number
2. Name of section/category

Sheet 2

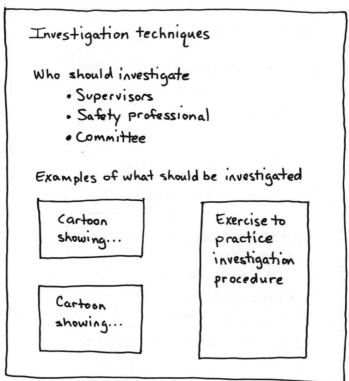

Sheet 3

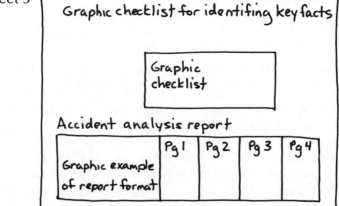

Figure 21–1. *(continued).*

Storyboarding for a Computer Manual

Step	Screen Will Say	What This Means
1. Enter decimal values.	What next?	Define decimal values.
2. Enter input file name.	Drive A or B?	Explanations about the original files.
3. Enter output file name.	Drive B or C?	Explanation of how output files are categorized.
4. Press ENTER	File name text	Program is offering opportunity to change selections. Explain the various selections.

Figure 21–2. Storyboarding for a computer manual. Storyboards help you visualize the sequence and the general outline of a manual before drafting it.

3. Headline
4. Summary of concept to be explained
5. Full text
6. Exhibits (screens, diagrams, tables, drawings)

Whichever storyboarding method you use, the basic idea is the same: You should visualize the development of each concept in the entire manual before you write a word of text. Storyboarding allows you to see the logical (or illogical) order of ideas, the repetition, the variety of visuals planned, and any missing information. With the "picture" of the entire manual before you, you can then rearrange concepts, add topics where you find gaps, break text with visuals where the paragraphing will look too solid, or provide more practice exercises or illustrations.

After you've looked at the entire manual "model" on your wall or desktop, you may decide to arrange these ideas into a linear outline—perhaps on your computer.

The next step in storyboarding is to get everybody's feedback on and approval of your plan. A storyboard plan or outline is much quicker to review than an entire manual draft—and much easier to revise and rearrange.

Missing information from your supervisor? Simply add another plan sheet with the skeleton idea.

The supervisor doesn't want to include idea K? Fine, you've wasted only a few minutes planning that concept, not hours drafting paragraphs of explanation. Simply remove the concept from your plan.

A good idea from a colleague for an analogy or graphic illustration? Pencil it on your storyboard so you won't forget it later as you draft the text.

Revisions are easy at this point. Incorporate any changes, additions, or deletions suggested by supervisors, colleagues, or other users, and then show them the modified storyboards for a second review. Ask them to formally sign off on your plan. If they do, chances are great that they'll be equally satisfied with your full draft.

Planning Effective Graphics

The "show, don't tell" principle was mentioned earlier. That principle applies especially to graphics you choose to illustrate your explanations and procedures. This book contains a complete section on graphic design (see **Part 4**). Here we want to emphasize only one important point about the graphics specifically found in manuals.

Some users refer to manuals only for the illustrations. That is, they read *none* of the text. Therefore, graphics that demonstrate key steps must be complete within themselves. They don't just supplement the written text; they should often duplicate it. Headings must make complete statements, not just contain key words. The skimming reader must be able to tell from the headline what the visual shows and what the main point is.

Finally, enlarge your concept of graphics. They are not simply drawings or pictures. Graphics may include flowcharts and process diagrams, screen displays, photos, drawings, dialogue scripts, role plays, or mathematical or statistical data. A graphic illustration is anything that further illuminates an idea in the written text.

Use graphics liberally in your manual.

Troubleshooting Table for a Manual

Error	May Be Caused by	To Correct
Error E11	Cursor is stuck to the left of the column.	Move the cursor so that it lies within range.
Error E12	Utility program is not installed.	Install Utility C3.
Error E13	The WSOVRR file is damaged.	Make a new copy from master disk.
Error E14	Database is too large for one file.	Exit from ZStar. Use ROPP to run the program.

Figure 21–3. Troubleshooting table for a manual. The trouble-shooting table allows readers to identify and correct their errors without having to wade through long paragraphs of complex explanation.

The Troubleshooting Section

When things go wrong, equipment operators, computer users, or class-room learners want to know how to find and correct the problem quickly, without having to read through pages and pages of text.

For that reason, manual writers should present troubleshooting assistance separately. Decision trees and troubleshooting tables are the most effective ways to give such information simply and painlessly (see **Figures 21–3** and **21–4**).

Drafting

When you have prepared storyboards for the entire manual and have had supervisors or colleagues review and sign off on them, you're ready to add meat to the skeleton. The drafting step is usually the fastest and the easiest because you already know what points you want to make and in what order to present them. In this phase, you're merely turning your key ideas (headlines and subheads) into sentences.

You can write the entire draft yourself or delegate portions of the writing to colleagues. Because each section is self-contained, you do not have to depend on the other writers to feed you information or duplicate your layout. The ideas and their presentation sequence have already been established and approved.

Troubleshooting Decision Tree for a Manual

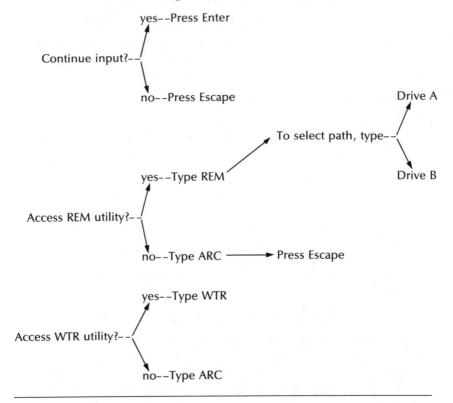

Figure 21–4. Troubleshooting decision tree for a manual. The decision tree gives readers an easy-to-visualize plan for tracing or retracing their actions.

Write the draft for each section as fast as you can—in one sitting if at all possible. Do not stop to make changes, to correct grammar, or to eliminate repetition. This drafting stage should require about 25 percent of your total writing time.

As you write, keep these suggestions in mind:

- Use plain English. Never use jargon to define jargon.
- Add analogies where you can.
- Explain how an object or procedure is like something else and how it differs.
- Establish rapport with your reader by using the "you" approach. Your writing will be clearer and more concise as a result.

Revising

The remaining 25 percent of the project involves revising the draft. If you have used storyboarding, you should not have to alter or rearrange concepts at this stage. You're simply revising paragraph and sentence structure.

The writing principles presented elsewhere in this book, particularly those in **Part 2**, should be helpful in doing the revision.

Updating

Your final consideration in manual design and writing is how to update and correct the manual: Company policies change, equipment models become obsolete, training course curricula need revision, software applications expand, and errors and weaknesses in the original manual surface.

Therefore, when you decide how to reproduce the manual (three-ring binder, glued binding, computer disk, hardcover book), keep the need for updating in mind.

When you find serious errors, weaknesses, or omissions, you can correct the master copy immediately and send out a notice to all users to change their copies immediately as well.

For minor updates and revisions, you may decide to keep a file of changes. When you accumulate several, send out to other users the updates and changes in a batch. Users are more likely to insert these changes and keep their manuals current if they are not bombarded daily or weekly with revisions.

Perhaps after a year, or three or four years, the manual changes have been so frequent and extensive as to require a new edition. If your master copy has been updated continually, the new edition will simply involve going back to the storyboarding stage, with much of the text draft already completed. You'll simply paste up unchanged parts of the old manual as a new skeleton and then add headlines and graphics for the new topics.

Manual writing is much like movie writing. Scriptwriters visualize the plot in scenes, from the opening murder to the car chase scene to the tearjerking finale in the hospital room. With the scenes in mind, adding the dialogue comes rather easily.

22

Correspondence

Common weaknesses in correspondence include buried key ideas, unclear expectations about the actions to be taken, and an impersonal, discourteous tone. Most technical correspondence should follow the MADE format: Message, Action, Details, Evidence. (Evidence, if any, consists of optional attachments or enclosures.)

Correspondence doesn't always communicate. A sales manager of a large computer company recently walked into a meeting where the latest communiqué from headquarters was under discussion. "That is the craziest, most absurd, most confusing memo I've ever read in my life." All the sales reps around the table agreed and expressed variations of that sentiment.

"Headquarters wrote us a memo supposedly to tell us how to calculate discount prices on trade-in equipment, but I gave up about half way through. I never did understand whether we were supposed to accept the equipment and offer the buy-back price ourselves. And understanding the calculations was impossible. What are we supposed to do with the memo anyway? I figure I'll just file it for the contact name and number and, if the subject ever comes up, call to ask somebody up there to translate."

The manager hit on the two most frequent complaints about internal correspondence: The key ideas are buried and the action to be taken is unclear. In other words, headquarters had just sent their sales department another typical "So what?" memo.

A third frequent complaint about letters and memos from technical professionals is that they are impersonal, abrupt, or even downright rude. In C. S. Forrester's series about British naval warfare around 1800, Captain Hornblower frequently received overbearing, curt dispatches and orders from the admiralty. We have seen correspondence from technicians to their supervisors or, worse, to customers that would rival those of Lord Cornwallis to his subordinates. Because their information is strictly factual, technical writers often pay too little attention to their tone and may sound overbearing, or even threatening. Remember that courtesy is always a virtue, even in technical writing.

The Ascending Format

Because letters are relatively short documents, technical writers tend to use the once-upon-a-time essay format they learned in English composition class. Their letters often begin with an account of what prompted them to write, continue with supporting details, and finally present the main points and conclusions.

With that arrangement, readers must forge ahead in the dark, unaware of the significance of those tidbits of information floating by. They continue to plow through detail after detail with a "So what's the point?" attitude until they finally get to the "Ah-ha" conclusion at the end of the letter. Then with that conclusion in mind, they have to go back to the beginning of the letter to re-sort and rethink the details that didn't quite make sense on first reading.

In other words, the letter has been written backward. (The remarks above apply to memos as well.)

The Descending Format

So what prevents this backward approach and helps readers understand the message and action on the first reading?

Many technical professionals are relieved to discover a format for writing effective informational letters: the MADE format.

Message	What is the message of most interest to your reader?
Action	What action do you want your reader to take? Or what follow-up action do you plan to take?
Details	Elaborate on the necessary details—who, what, when, where, why, how, how much?
Evidence	Mention any attachments or enclosures that will make the message clearer or the action easier to take.

Review the memos in **Figures 22–1** and **22–2** to see how much easier it is to understand the message on the first reading when a document is in the MADE format.

Note that a message statement differs from a purpose statement. Many writers have learned from the experience of reading the documents of others that finding the key points up front helps. But the message statement in the MADE format (see **Figure 22–2**) goes much further than a purpose statement.

A purpose statement contains hints about the general subject and promises to give important information later in the memo or letter. A message statement actually informs; it gives the key information, the meat of your idea (see **Section 1.1** for more examples).

Purpose Statement:

> This memo will address the issue of contracting with Belton Labs as a sole-source supplier for our lab needs.

Message Statement:

> Belton Labs has offered us discount prices on our routine lab supplies. If we deal with them as a sole-source contractor, we can save approximately $100,000 next year on our routine supplies.

Purpose Statement:

> This memo will outline increases in the June oil production values on the Fortenberry tract.

Message Statement:

> Oil production on the Fortenberry tract has increased 80 percent during June. The most remarkable increases have been in four of the five wells treated with chemical injections.

For excellent examples of message statements that give the big picture in summary form, see the one-paragraph summaries in the "What's News?" column of the *Wall Street Journal*. Those paragraphs are so informative that many subscribers never read the full-length stories.

You should allow your own readers to control their reading time in the same way. They should be able to read as much or as little as necessary to find out what they need to know to do their jobs. Their interest in your subject should dictate how much they need to read; they should not find themselves a captive audience to a long-winded rambler. If they stop reading your memo or letter early, they should still come away with the main idea.

To summarize: The MADE format works for two primary reasons—clarity and reading time.

There are, however, a few cases where the MADE format is perhaps not ideal, for example, a memo or letter of refusal. When telling someone no, presenting that negative message up front may be too abrupt and harsh. When that's the case, you may prefer to begin with a positive or neutral statement, build up to the negative message by giving the reasons for your decision, and finally state your refusal at the end.

But for most correspondence on technical matters, use the MADE format for communicating your ideas effectively.

Once-Upon-a-Time Correspondence

To:

From:

Subject: KEW De-oiling Heater Options

So?
What do you want me to do!

Attached are calculations showing the cost of a serious de-oiling heater problem. The pressure drop through the KEW de-oiling heater has caused operations to bypass the heater and go to the soft-wax recovery surge drum to prevent dewaxing filter boots from overflowing. According to my calculations, the old boot pumps can run 6590 BPD at 221 feet of head with new impellers. New impellers from Huffmaster are available on 26-week delivery. These impellers have a capacity of 7100 BPD at 200 feet of head. On certain blocks it would be necessary to run 7200 BPD at 210 feet of head, so new pumps would definitely help overcome the pressure-drop problem.

So?

The control valve is oversized and does not contribute to the pressure-drop problem. The de-oiling heater has plenty of warming area, but the treated water side is fouled and needs cleaning.

There are four permanent solutions to the problem:

Which one is best?

1. Replace the de-oiling heater with a larger one.
2. Add another heater in parallel.
3. Replace the boot pumps with a surge drum and two large pumps.
4. Replace the impellers in the boot pumps.

Oh, I see.

We recommend the surge drum and new pumps mentioned in the Process Duty Specification. We also recommend that the de-oiling heater be carefully designed with a high fluid-flow velocity because melting product wax adversely affects filtering.

Here's where I come in. Of course I'll call!

As you know, this procedure is costly because part of the bypass material is product wax. We need your decision about either replacing or adding another de-oiling heater. Please call me with any further questions.

Figure 22–1. Once-upon-a-time correspondence. The reader must read to the end of this memo before the details make complete sense and the recommendations become clear.

MADE Format Correspondence

To:

From:

Subject: KEW De-oiling Heater Options

Message {
Due to the pressue drop through the KEW de-oiling heater, product wax is bypassing to the soft-wax recovery surge drum. This problem leads to a loss of approximately $10,000 annually.
}

Action recommended {
To correct this problem, we recommend the purchase and installation of a new surge drum and pumps to replace the existing dewax boot pumps. This change will solve the problem permanently without causing damage to the wax crystal. We also recommend a de-oiling heater with a high fluid-flow velocity be installed because melting product wax reduces filtering efficiency and increases pressure drop.
}

Details how much {
The total cost of these changes will be $4200. The project can be completed by September 1, with a total downtime of three days or less.

The other three possible solutions are:
}

Details how else {
• Replace the de-oiling heater with a larger one.

• Add another heater in parallel.

• Replace the impellers in the boot pumps.
}

The old boot pumps can run only 6590 BPD at 221 feet of head with new impellers. Larger impellers have a delivery wait of over 26 weeks, a delay that will mean the problem cannot be corrected before winter. Furthermore, the maximum capacity of the existing pumps is 7100 BPD at 200 feet of head, and on certain blocks it will be necessary to run 7200 BPD at 210 feet of head. Thus, new pumps will be necessary anyway. Additionally, new pumps will definitely help overcome the pressure-drop problem.

The control valve is oversized and does not contribute to the pressure-drop problem. The de-oiling heater has plenty of warming area, but the treated water side is fouled and needs cleaning. This cleaning will be done during downtime for modifications.

Evidence {
As you know, the present situation is very costly because part of the bypass material is product wax. Attached are calculations detailing the cost of the problem.
}

Figure 22–2. MADE format correspondence. By having the message and action statements up front, the reader can understand the details on first reading.

205

23

Papers and
Journal Articles

23.1   Why and Where to Publish

Publishing professional articles brings money, recognition, and customers or clients to your doorstep. To determine what should be the slant of your article, you should study the business or professional journals in which you want to publish.

Never mind that we have all seen articles that were mainly useful for lining canary cages. Nothing enhances your credibility or brings recognition—from colleagues, from your own management, from customers and clients—like publishing an article or book on your subject of expertise. This principle has even worked its way into the language: To establish a person's credibility, we say, "She wrote the book."

Why Publish?

Recognition and credibility aside, one reason to publish is money. Although professional journals rarely pay authors for contributing articles, business publications do offer fees, sometimes as much as $2,000–$3,000. Technical book authors, of course, earn royalties and may make anywhere from a few hundred to thousands of dollars.

And when you consider the new business generated by published papers and books, even nonpaying journals "pay." In fact, the return rate on reader-response cards can be as high as 2–3 percent, a direct measure of the new business generated by published articles. When such articles bring new clients for the organization, more recognition, perhaps even corporate bonus money, trickles down to the author.

Legal considerations can also be a motivation for publishing. Organizations or individuals may want to publish their research or their work to "go on record" within the industry as having been the first to have completed some significant, specific research or task.

Others publish to record their development for the archival value, to propose a new program or process to their peers, to instruct others in new developments or principles, or to satisfy academic requirements.

Prestige, money, new business, recognition—all are valuable and reasonable to expect as a result of publishing your work.

Choice of Publications

So where do you start?

Your first choice for submission of your article will usually be one of the business or trade publications you regularly read. Through the months and years, you have probably observed what kinds of articles these periodicals present and what the editorial viewpoints seem to be. You have also probably picked up other miscellaneous bits of information, such as what kinds of leads, headings, titles, and graphics they prefer.

But if the journals you read do not publish the kind of article you have in mind or if you prefer to publish in a more prestigious publication, do further research to find a home for your article.

A primary source for internationally published professional journals and business and trade publications is *Ulrich's International Periodical Directory*, put out by R. R. Bowker. Another source is *Standard Rate and Data Service*, which lists business publications and other media. The latter also carries advertising rates, markets served, and demographic and geographic editions published. Finally, of course, most professional organizations have listings of major publications of interest to their members.

Whether you choose a business or professional journal will be determined by the audience you want to reach. Business journals are primarily read by nonexperts in a particular field. Professional journals are read by specialists. Depending on which kind of publication you choose, you will slant your article to either nonexperts or other technical experts like yourself.

Once you decide whether to direct your article toward experts or nonexperts, you should narrow your choices further by asking the following questions about particular journals:

- Who are its readers?
- Does it publish articles on this subject?
- What trends is it following?
- What is its acceptance-to-publication lead time?
- For what departments, categories, special issues, or special columns would this subject be appropriate?
- What is the average length of the typical article?
- Do the articles contain jargon or are they written for the general lay reader?
- Is the tone didactic, self-promoting, informative?
- What is the style of the typical article? (Case study? Theory? How to?)
- What is the format of the typical article? (Abstracts? Introductions? Illustrations? Sentence and paragraph length? Headings?)

- Does the publication use graphics? What kind?

Answers to these questions will help you narrow your choices to probably three or four publications. Once you've determined which ones, start by sending your article to one of the following, depending on your reason for publishing:

- The most prestigious one
- The one with the largest circulation (consider pass-on readership)
- The one that is read by the client or customer base you want to reach

If your paper is rejected by the first one, work your way down the list.

Publication and the accompanying recognition are well worth the effort. And because magazines and journals are constantly searching for good material, you may find that being published is not as difficult as you think.

23.2 Query Letters

The purpose of a query letter to an editor is to request permission to send a complete manuscript. It tells an editor (1) what your subject is and how you plan to handle it, (2) how long the article will be and approximately when it will be completed, and (3) what your credentials are.

A query is a business letter sent to an editor to prepare the way for submission of a full-length paper. The query saves time for both editor and author.

Why Send a Query?

Why shouldn't a writer just send a complete article? First-time authors frequently ask this question, so it's important to understand how a query letter benefits both editor and would-be author.

Many editors prefer them because letters save them time. They need to read only one page rather than the entire manuscript to tell whether they'd be interested in your paper. To find a particular editor's preference about queries, look through past issues of the journal for an editorial article entitled "Manuscript Submissions," "Criteria for Publishing," or "Editorial Guidelines," or the like. Guidelines are usually published once a year in these journals to tell writers how to submit their papers. If you can't locate this edition, phone the editorial assistant for a copy.

Queries will save you time.　If you can find no editor who is interested in publishing your subject, then you've saved yourself the effort and time of writing the article.

Queries get faster responses from the editor than complete manuscripts. Usually a query will get an answer within 5 to 10 days. A complete manuscript may sit on someone's desk for weeks or months before it's read and evaluated.

Queries help you tailor the paper to the editor's preferences.　He or she may want to suggest a particular slant, length, or arrangement, particular additions or omissions, specific kinds of graphics, or an abstract.

Although the query letter makes publishing a two-step process for you, the benefits far outweigh the effort required to prepare the letter.

What to Include in a Query

In a query, you should state your subject and how you plan to present it; discuss nuts-and-bolts matters such as format, length, and completion date; and explain who you are and why you are qualified to write on this subject. In addition to your technical qualifications, editors will be interested in your writing style. Therefore, if you have published previously, by all means say so and send a clipping as a writing sample. Effective queries which rarely are more than a page, should include the following parts.

Subject.　Summarize the subject of your paper in two to four sentences, being as specific as you can. If possible, try to arouse interest with a subject hook—in much the same way that articles in popular business and general interest magazines do.

Title.　Mention the title of your paper and keep in mind that you want to arouse the reader's interest. Rarely is the title you would use for an internal report to management appropriate as a published title. Revise titles that begin "Description of," "An Analysis of," or "An Examination of." Try to indicate how the reader will benefit by delving into your paper. Keep in mind, however, that if your article is accepted, the editor may change the title.

The Handle.　Tell the editor how you plan to handle your subject. Some editors slant their articles to management readers, some to theoreticians, some to general practitioners. Identify your general audience and your method of presentation. Is it a how-to article? A theoretical article? An introduction to new technology? An introduction to a new application? A case history of how your organization or another handled something? A survey of expert opinions? A survey of the person on the street? A historical panorama? An agree/disagree argument? Presentation of a problem and solution?

Here is where your study of past journal issues will be invaluable in shaping your letter. You don't want to waste your time and the editor's in sending a theoretical presentation to a journal that publishes only how-to manuscripts. Studying the publication before submission is a common principle in publishing, but it's too often overlooked by those who hope to publish.

Key-Topic Outline: Briefly mention two or three of your key points, either in paragraph form or with a bulleted list. Give the editor enough so that he or she can understand the substance and significance of your subject.

Credentials. Tell why you are qualified to write on the proposed subject. Include your present work and accomplishments, your job title and employer's name, major customers or clients involved with the work, your education, any awards, and any publishing credits.

Nuts and Bolts: The nuts-and-bolts section contains any miscellaneous comments or questions about the paper's publication. Generally, you'll give the editor answers to the following questions: Approximately what length (number of words) will the manuscript be? Are photos or other graphics available? Will you include an abstract? Has the paper been published elsewhere? How long will it take you to complete the paper after the editor gives you the go-ahead? (It's generally unwise to name a specific date because different journals work with different lead times. Instead, say something like, "I can complete the manuscript in six weeks from your response to my query.")

Permission to Send the Article. Finally, ask the editor if he or she is interested in seeing the proposed manuscript.

Figure 23–1 presents a model query to a publisher.

If you decide to phone an editor rather than write, you can present the same information as previously outlined. One caution, however, about querying over the phone: To do so may be a waste of time for both you and the editor. First, some journal editors will return prospective authors' phone calls; others prefer letters and will not return such calls. Second, it is difficult to convey the essence of your article in a short conversation. Editors have no way of judging your writing abilities in a phone call. They may express interest in

---

Query Letter to a Publisher

April 4, 19—

Dear Ms. Felton:

You've probably come across specimens of grain sizes that look like the samples I've enclosed. Metallographers and others in the metals industry have been perplexed about these variations and have looked for a way to deal with them for years. I'd like to prepare an article entitled "Characterizing Duplex Grain Sizes" that presents a new classification standard and explains its intent.

The article will include:

- A definition of "duplex grain size"
- a determination of variances
- two basic classifications—random and topological variances
- four procedures for precision measurements

The manuscript should run about 2,000–2,500 words. Of course, drawings of specimens (such as the ones enclosed) will accompany the text. The paper could be completed in about a month after receipt of your expression of interest.

At present, I am a senior technical representative with Vivco Alloys, Inc. in Casper, Wyoming. At other companies I have worked for during the past 16 years, I have also been involved in the research, development, and production of nickel alloys, including both wrought and mechanically alloyed materials. For the past 18 months, as chairman of Project Group R0933 of Committee RO on Metallography, I've been heavily involved in developing specifications for these same materials.

Would you be interested in seeing the above described article? A stamped, self-addressed envelope is enclosed for your reply.

Sincerely,

Figure 23–1. Query letter to a publisher. Query letters save time and effort for both editors and authors.

---

your subject, but, after you spend time preparing the article, reject your manuscript simply because it's poorly written. The query letter will provide that important writing sample.

Writing a query is time well spent for both writer and editor. The only time a query letter is inappropriate is when the piece of writing is a very short filler (two to three pages) for a column or consists primarily of photos, with only a brief accompanying text.

23.3   Criteria for Publication

Editors and review boards select papers for publication based on the following reasons: to report new developments on existing practices or products, to present expert opinion to keep readers better informed, to give details of proprietary work underway, to instruct readers, and to present newsworthy events and issues related to the industry.

Rarely is an editor totally responsible for decisions about papers accepted for publication in his or her journal. Most editors depend on an editorial review committee composed of various technical experts. The committee will review a paper and express opinions about the idea, the timeliness of the subject, the method of presentation, and the style of writing. The reviewers express their opinions to the editor, and then the editor makes the final decision on acceptance or rejection.

Does that mean the editor publishes what he or she pleases? Hardly. The editor must please the journal's readership or the publication will gradually be shunned by colleagues in the field.

Do advertisers carry weight in the decision whether to accept? That depends on how you look at it. Yes, some organizations that place ads in a journal get papers by their staff published. However, advertisers *are* part of the industry. They show interest, invest in research, and instruct readers, and they should rightly be considered part of the industry's readership. Editors do react negatively, however, to subtle and not-so-subtle bribes—that is, when authors send manuscripts with promises to advertise in the journal.

Do those in PR have a better chance of getting something published than others? Again, the answer is yes and no. They do not carry more weight because they are associated with or retained by a major company, but they do tend to get articles placed because they know what good press releases should and should not do. Press releases are newsworthy notices that should not blantantly sell a product, service, or company. They may quote key company representatives and interview customers and clients using the product or service, but the focus of the press release is the newsworthy event, product, discovery, or issue.

An editor's final decision for publication must rest on his or her responsibility to report new developments on existing practices or products, to present expert opinions to keep readers better informed, to give details of proprietary work underway, to instruct readers, and to present newsworthy events and issues related to the industry.

23.4 Manuscript Preparation, Permissions or Approvals, and Rights

The physical appearance of your manuscript is a reflection of your work. Prepared and submitted appropriately, the manuscript establishes credibility for your ideas; prepared carelessly, it has little or no chance of publication.

Editors continually complain about receiving article or book manuscripts that resemble technical reports to management or doctoral dissertations. Yet, such carelessness (or naivete) is surprising, because each manuscript creates a lasting impression of the author's attitude toward his or her research and work.

Every manuscript sent to an editor should be considered a sales tool (to gain acceptance) and should be treated as such. The following guidelines on manuscript preparation should move your manuscript from the mediocre to the outstanding pile.

Preparation of Press Releases

Address a press release to the general editor; he or she will either route it or discard it.

A press release should contain all the essential information, with no need for a cover letter. The release should be typed double-spaced on standard $8\frac{1}{2}" \times 11"$ or $8\frac{1}{2}" \times 14"$ paper. Any photos to be enclosed should be the standard $4" \times 5"$ or $5" \times 7"$ size, with a notation of that enclosure on the release itself. The contact name and phone number should be located in either the upper left or right corner. At the bottom of each page that is continued, the word *more* should appear. The symbol ### should be typed after the last line of the release. (See **Figure 23–2** for a model.)

Preparation of Paper and Article Manuscripts

Unless the specific journal guidelines instruct you otherwise, type your manuscript double-spaced on clean, regular $8\frac{1}{2}" \times 11"$ bond paper. Leave margins of about $1"$ to $1\frac{1}{2}"$ on all sides. Never add fancy borders or artwork on the title page or cover. Never staple manuscript pages together. Clip them loosely.

Model Press Release

For immediate release [*Or:* For release after June 2]

Contact: Cheryl Smith
 (233)459-4893

Enclosure: Photo of laser printer

TITLE GOES HERE

Text begins here...

....

....

(more)

Page 2

Text continues. ....

....

.... ends.

\# \# \#

Figure 23–2. Model press release. Press releases should follow the standard format.

On the title page include the article title and an abstract (if required). If the abstract is a lengthy one, begin it on the second page. In your cover letter and in the upper left corner of the title page, include contact information: your name, address, company affiliation, and phone number. In the upper right corner, type the approximate word count of the manuscript. (The average manuscript page should contain 250–300 words.) On the bottom of the title page or on a separate page, include a brief biographical sketch that can be used along with your byline.

Although editors have the final say about titles, headings, and abstract blurbs, include these in your manuscript when you submit it. They will simply make the editor's job easier if he or she decides to publish your work.

Put a heading at the top of each page (your name or the manuscript title) for identification purposes in case the pages become separated during the editorial review process. However, if the journal passes on blind submissions to the editorial review board, be careful *not* to include your name or that of any coauthor on the manuscript pages. These pages can then be detached from the title page and circulated to various readers for their opinions about publication. (Editors differ on whether to let their reviewers know who the author is.)

Some journals request that you send multiple copies, usually three, of your manuscript. Most articles, even those rejected, will not be returned, so be sure to keep extra copies in your files. Use a large envelope for mailing; do not fold the manuscript pages, no matter how short the article.

Some magazines will prepare graphics from your sketches. Others will not. If you are writing for the latter, enclose the graphics but separate them from the text. Provide a page listing all the graphics and their captions so they can be reinserted if misplaced. Be sure each graphic itself has a number and a complete, informative title. Use stiffeners if necessary for protection, and roll oversized graphics rather than fold them. For identification purposes—but outside the area to be reproduced—designate the "top" of each graphic and add your name and phone number. Number only manuscript pages, not artwork pages.

If the journal publishes author photos (many business journals do), include a 5" × 7" black-and-white glossy photo, with your name, address, and phone number on the back to avoid interference with reprinting.

If you did not prepare a query letter to establish contact with an editor and determine his or her interest in your idea (see **Section 23.2**), now is the time to find the name of the appropriate editor. If you can't find the name on past issues of the journal, phone to ask which editor handles articles on your subject and get the correct spelling of the name.

In packaging your manuscript and artwork for submission, be sure to mark the outside envelope "Requested Manuscript" to bypass the slush pile of unsolicited manuscripts that may have been lying for months on someone's desk waiting to be reviewed.

Requested Changes in the Manuscript

Many editors will forward your manuscript to two or perhaps three "expert" reviewers for their opinions about acceptance. The reviews may or may not be blind. Some editors want a manuscript always to be evaluated on its own merits—its contribution to the field, time-liness, accuracy, and style. Other editors consider it important that the reviewer know the author in making an evaluation. In either case, editors have the final say in whether to accept the article for publication. They may pass the reviewer's actual comments on to you or present them in summary by phone or letter. Such specific comments can often help you improve the article for resubmission to that journal (if some interest was indicated) or for submission elsewhere.

Occasionally, the editor may accept the article on the condition that you make certain changes in the manuscript. At that point, you can (1) make the requested changes, (2) defend your original manuscript and explain why you think the requests are invalid, or (3) withdraw your manuscript from consideration.

Permission or Approvals

Include with your article all necessary permissions for quoted or reprinted materials and any bylines for artwork. For some manuscripts that include proprietary information or that will possibly create legal difficulties, it may be necessary to get senior executives in your organization to sign off on the manuscript submission. Include any such sign-offs or other releases, such as those granting permission for you to mention the name of another person or organization in the article.

Keep copies of all these permissions and sign-offs for your own files in case of later legal difficulties.

Rights

Be very careful to tell an editor if the material has appeared anywhere else and, if so, in what publication, in what country, in what issue, and on what date. The journal may or may not be interested in reprinting your article under those circumstances, depending on the overlap in readership. This is the kind of information you will include in a query letter (see **Section 23.2**), but you should also repeat it when submitting the final manuscript.

Editors will usually want first-time rights, although contracts of acceptance often specify exclusive world rights. Once the manuscript is accepted, you can negotiate to have the rights returned to you for reprints or other uses such as sending copies to prospective clients. Most publications will have no objection to returning these rights to you.

Following publishing protocol is important for your personal and corporate image. The rewards of publishing can be tremendous in terms of prestige and new business.

Part 4

Effective Visuals

24

Selecting and Designing Effective Visuals

24.1   When and When Not to Use Visuals

Visuals save reading time, simplify text, make abstract terms understandable, emphasize key points, summarize facts and trends, and present ideas creatively so that readers remember them.

Visuals are both the message and the medium. Correctly used as a message, they displace text and explain ideas better than words themselves—simplifying, clarifying, and summarizing. As a medium, visuals highlight key points and create high-impact pictures that remain in the reader's memory.

Many people "digest" a report simply by reading the abstract or executive summary and then by looking at the tables and figures. If readers can grasp the important ideas with such little effort, why shouldn't they? Why should they have to read tedious textual passages when they can understand the significant information with a quick glance at a graphic presentation? Visuals require much less conceptualizing time from the reader.

An additional benefit of visuals is that they make facts or statistics more explicit and memorable by showing relationships. They tell readers how to interpret the data—what the facts or numbers mean.

Consider the impact of visuals this way: How effective would advertisers be if they presented their new products by rolling paragraphs of text across the TV screen?

On the other hand, some writers approach the question of visuals haphazardly and wind up adding far too many, simply because they find them easy to create with the aid of computers. Journal editors in particular begin to frown when they receive an article with too many graphics, because they are expensive to prepare for publication.

Use the following checklist to cull unnecessary visuals from your presentation:

- Does the visual emphasize trivial or irrelevant information?

- Can the information be included in another visual without cluttering it?

- Does the information confuse rather than clarify?

- Has the information already been included simply and emphatically in the text?

24.2   Visuals Based on Concept

To be effective, each visual should have one primary purpose; that purpose dictates the most appropriate visual design.

Most technical professionals tend to select the same visual designs repeatedly. Yet because there are so many ways to present data graphically, the challenge is to decide which is the most effective choice for which concept. Choosing the wrong visuals for your information is like wearing a tuxedo to McDonald's.

Figure 24–1 lists the primary purposes for the most frequently used visuals.

Let's look in detail at some of the most common visuals.

Bar or Column Charts

A bar chart has horizontal bars (**Figure 24–2**); a column chart has vertical bars (**Figure 24–3**). Such charts best show data groupings and percentages. They also add impact to high/low comparisons. Data can be sequenced in a variety of ways: numerically, chronologically, geographically, qualitatively, or progressively. Data in vertical bars can be more easily compared than data in horizontal bars. Additionally, vertical bars or columns also provide more room for labels.

Bar or column charts are meaningless, however, when the differences between quantities are small. Newspaper editors are fond of splitting the vertical scale on column charts (or the horizontal scale on bar charts). This split makes the absolute difference between quantities much more apparent. Technical writers should avoid this practice because it often creates a graphic that misrepresents relative differences, which, after all, is what you're trying to show with a bar or column chart. If you must use a split scale, make sure to point out that fact clearly on the graphic.

Line Graph

A line graph emphasizes movement and change over time. Generally, the independent variable is shown on the horizontal axis and the dependent variable is shown on the vertical axis. Line graphs quickly become cluttered when you try to convey too much information or present too much variation.

Line graphs are not often useful for presenting quantitative data, but they are unsurpassed for showing trends (see **Figure 24–4**).

Visuals Based on Concept

Visual	Best Illustrates
bar or column chart	relative quantities
line graph	trends to be compared over a long period; to emphasize movement rather than amounts
circle graph	proportions of a whole
flowchart or time chart	a process through steps or stages
map	locations
line drawing	a simple phase of a process or an enlargement of physical detail
stepchart	a procedure
diagram	how something looks or works
network	how events or persons are related
table	body of data
pictorial	comparison of units
organizational chart	relationships between positions
decision tree	steps involving actions or decisions
cluster	related ideas within a whole
matrix	comparisons
cartoon	abstract ideas
photo	how something looks

Figure 24–1. Visuals based on concept. Choose a visual appropriate to the concept and your purpose.

Horizontal Bar Chart

Revenue Distribution by Manufacturing Location

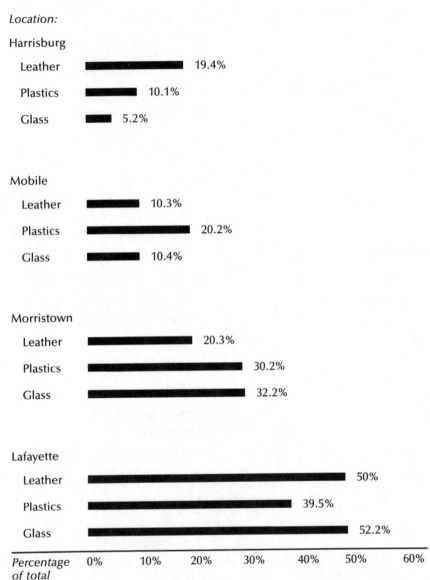

Figure 24–2. Horizontal bar chart. Such a chart allows quick understanding of multifaceted comparisons.

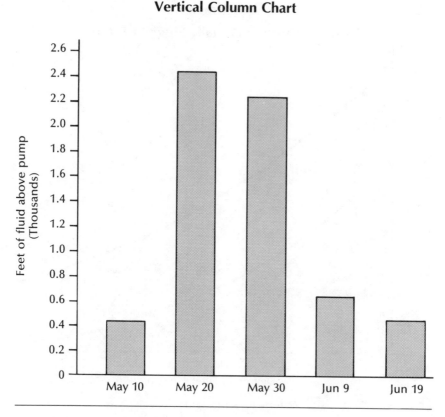

Figure 24–3. Vertical column chart. Such a chart emphasizes high/low comparisons.

Line graphs intended to show the results of data measurement should usually show each data point so the reader can draw conclusions about the precision of the relationship being shown. Line graphs showing trends need not show individual data points.

Circle Graph

A circle graph conveys data quickly and makes abstract percentages immediately visual as parts of a whole, as shown in **Figure 24–5**. A circle graph has little value in showing a large number of small percentages. Such graphs can present only a limited amount of data, and no part of the information can be updated without restructuring the entire graph.

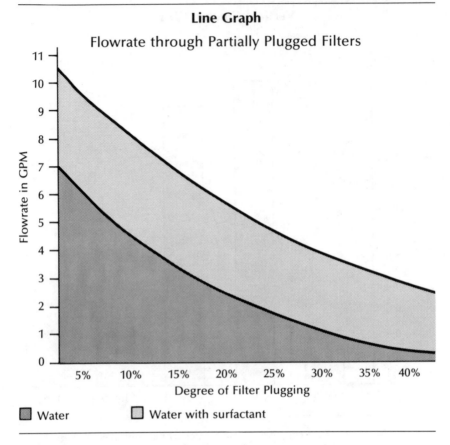

Figure 24–4. Line graph. These graphs emphasize movement of trends more than actual amounts.

Flowcharts

Flowcharts illustrate specific procedures, activities, or events as they proceed through often overlapping stages. The primary emphasis is on the movement, the interaction, and the sequences between stages (**Figure 24–6**). Cause-and-effect relationships can be presented quite effectively here. Unlike the circle graph, the bar or column chart, and the line graph, the flowchart looks complex and requires more concentration and time from the reader.

Logic flowcharts (as in **Figure 24–7**), which can show events, decisions, and alternate paths, are extremely useful in planning. Their primary use is in organizing complete activities, not necessarily in presenting specific schedules. Such charts also help ensure that all important points are addressed.

Circle Graph

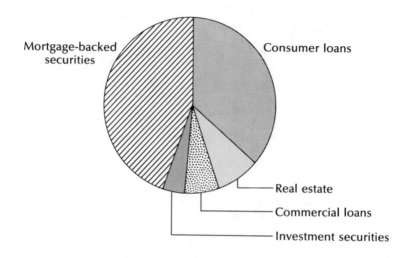

Distribution of Available Funds

Mortgage-backed securities

Consumer loans

Real estate

Commercial loans

Investment securities

Figure 24–5. Circle graph. Circle graphs best illustrate relationships of parts to a whole.

The Gantt flowchart, shown in **Figure 24–8**, was developed by Henry L. Gantt as a project management tool to effectively display the schedules of complex interactive and sequential events. In a Gantt chart, one axis shows output and the other axis shows units of time.

Map

A map, of course, shows location, but unless the preparer adds other effects to emphasize and highlight, readers may miss key points. Dots, symbols, pictures, shading, color, arrows, concentric circles, and spot blowups all add variety to a map and convey information easily and quickly. (See **Figure 24–9**.)

Drawings

Drawings may be more effective than photos to show the physical appearance or the inner workings of equipment or to illustrate a

Procedure Flowchart

Procedure for Monthly ERP Entries

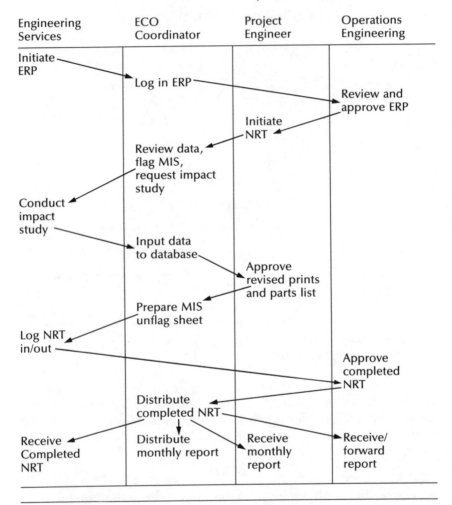

Figure 24–6. Procedure flowchart. These flowcharts emphasize interaction and cause-and-effect relationships.

process (See **Figure 24–10**). You should not try to show everything in a drawing; instead a drawing should be as simple as possible so it does not hide the key ideas you want to present. Informative labeling also helps readers grasp the major ideas quickly.

Logic Flowchart

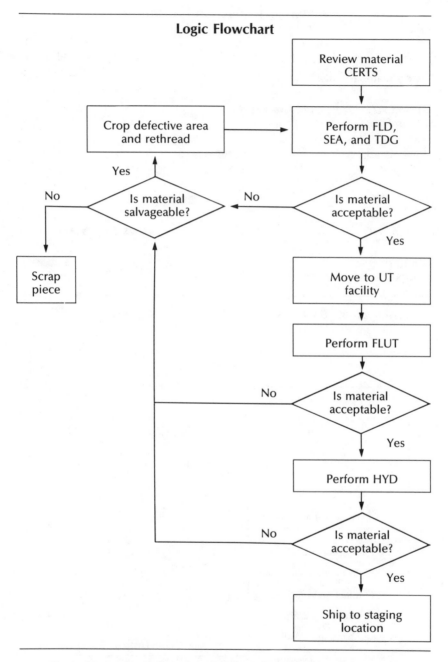

Figure 24–7. Logic flowchart. These flowcharts show not only sequential events, but also alternative paths that depend on the outcome of events. Rectangles indicate a process or activity, diamonds show where a decision must be made, and arrows indicate flow.

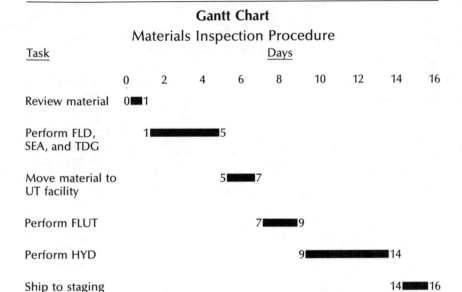

Figure 24–8. Gantt chart. These flowcharts effectively show schedules as well as interactions.

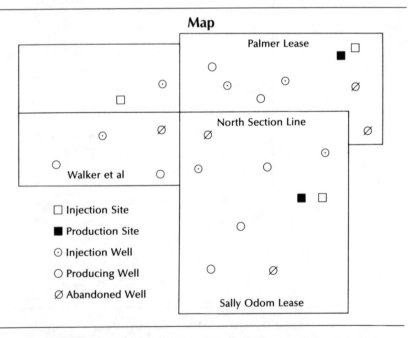

Figure 24–9. Map. Add variety to a map for easy and quick understanding of data.

Line Drawing

On the Spot Testing of Welds

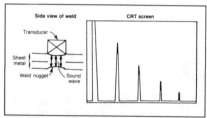

Ideal weld: double-spaced echoes; high attenuation (short echo); short echo train.

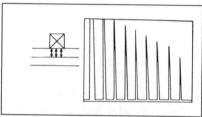

Worst case—no weld: single-spaced echoes; low attenuation (tall echo); long echo train.

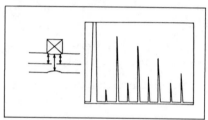

Marginal weld—undersized nugget: single spacing appearing between double-spaced echoes; low attenuation; long echo train.

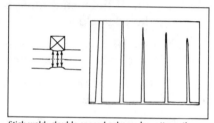

Stick weld: double-spaced echoes; low attenuation; long echo train.

Reprinted with permission from Tony Midora, "On the Spot Testing of Welds," *Mechanical Engineering Magazine*, September 1987, p. 78.

Figure 24–10. Line drawing. Line drawings can be more effective than photos to illustrate simple processes or the inner workings of equipment.

24.3 Guidelines for Design

A poorly designed visual is much worse than no visual at all.

1. Provide a reference in the text for every visual.

2. Place a visual that highlights new or significant information as close to its text reference as possible.

3. Place a visual containing reference data (that is, data of interest to only a few secondary readers) in an appendix, where it is easily accessible but does not clutter the text.

4. Group "lost" text passages (scattered text of only a few lines) together, placing multiple large visuals together at the end of the document or in a particular section.

5. Arrange visuals that are part of a series on a single page.

6. Retain the standard margins of the text.

7. Balance each visual on the page.

8. Never place a visual so that it is upside down when the reader holds it in the normal reading position or when the "gutter" (space in the middle of two bound pages) is at the top. If the visual must be sideways, the reader should turn the page clockwise to see it.

9. Set off each visual from the text by adequate white space, borders, or typeface changes or by using separate pages.

10. Give enough information within each visual so that it can stand alone.

11. Make wording on a visual consistent with the wording in the text reference.

12. Number visuals consecutively. Place them in the order in which they are referenced in the text.

13. If possible, present no more than one concept in each visual.

14. Give each visual an informative title and/or caption. Many readers will read only the captions and skim the text. Explain in the caption what the visual is illustrating (for example, not "Close-up of fatigue crack," but "Fatigue crack at 1000× shows transgranular propagation and planar shape").

15. Label all axes and columns.

16. Place labels in a straight and horizontal plane.

17. Be accurate and precise in the use of scales of measurement and in the wording of labels.

18. Prefer horizontal to vertical patterns and lines.

19. Arrange headings so the major classifications for ultimate comparison will be in vertical columns, not horizontal rows.

20. Use vertical lines for the strongest emphasis.

21. Express fractions as decimals.

22. Prefer standard symbols.

23. Give the sources of all data that are not your own.

24. Place legends, sources, or references within the body of the visual itself unless it would look too cluttered.

Part 5

The Editorial Relationship Between Managers and Technical Professionals

25

What Help
Should a Manager Give?

> *Managers should manage, not write or rewrite, their subordinates' documents. Management of the writing process includes giving background information, adequate time, and clear deadlines; providing necessary resources; and insisting on periodic reviews. If a manager wants certain points emphasized, he or she should make that known early in the writing process.*

Writing encompasses analyzing and planning a document as well as actually drafting it. Editing involves marking unclear or grammatically incorrect phraseology and raising questions about vague or missing ideas, gaps in logic, or inaccuracies. Rewriting is a complete redoing, possibly involving the addition or deletion of ideas, changes in structure or format, and sentence reconstruction.

The manager's role is primarily to edit the work of the technical support staff, not to write or rewrite. Managers who confuse these tasks find themselves frustrated because they're spending far too much time on tasks they thought they had delegated to their subordinates. Likewise, subordinates who work for such managers become equally frustrated when their work is returned to them in a barely recognizable form.

So how often does this happen? Too frequently. When customizing our writing workshop for a client, our instructors ask for writing samples of participants ahead of the workshop date so we can examine their weaknesses and tailor the course accordingly. New instructors are usually surprised when they receive a batch of these writing samples in the mail. They come to us and say, "These reports look pretty good! I don't think these people really need this course."

The situation is this: *The reports have all been rewritten by higher-level managers.* They resemble the first drafts in no way. In fact, when instructors distribute these samples in the workshop, the writer-owners sometimes cannot recognize their own reports!

Needless to say, writers and managers are frustrating each other over the writing-editing-rewriting process. Technical professionals cannot improve their writing when managers take no time to explain why they made the changes they did. In fact, some writers never see their rewrites at all and get absolutely no feedback on their work. How can they possibly improve for the next writing project?

Although managers may know what they *don't want* when they see it, they're often at a loss to explain what they *do want* in a report. In fact, sometimes they hide the very information that a writer must have to write an effective document. To see improvement, however, these managers must communicate clear directives to their technical writers. The following guidelines should help managers supervise the overall writing process.

Present the Plan

Assigning a report, a manual, or any other major writing project should not be done lightly—on the way out the door to lunch while discussing where to get the best burger. Without answers to key questions, writers will be working blindfolded. Therefore, when assigning a major writing project, always provide answers to the following questions:

- Who are the primary readers? What hidden audiences will there be?
- What is the purpose of the document?
- What will be the main interest of every reader in seeing and using the document?
- How much do the primary and secondary readers know about the subject?
- Are there personal or situational problems to consider? How should the writer handle these?
- Do you want simply an informational report or do you want a recommendation for action or for a decision?
- What are your criteria for making this recommendation?
- How do you rank the criteria? Which is most important? Least important?
- Are you willing to review the writing outline to suggest deletions, additions, or other changes before a complete draft is ready?
- How will you know if the document has been effective?
- When do you want the outline? The draft? The final document?

Give Ample Time and Clear Deadlines

It's quite unfair to a writer who has done extensive research to be given a sudden surprise deadline for a report on that work. A shoddy, inadequate report makes his or her entire research project seem insignificant or inadequately completed.

Allow your writer the time to document his or her work fully. And that means including a cooling-off period. Writers should have time to put their work aside for a few days (or better, a week or two) so they can come back to it with a fresh perspective. Only after such a cooling-off period will they be able to spot missing or inaccurate information, gaps in logic, inadequate emphasis, or weak sentence structure.

Provide Resources

Make clear to your staff what resources are available for use in meeting the deadline. Will there be graphic support from the art department? Will there be additional typists assigned to the project? Will the writer have unlimited access to the computer? Will there be a budget for extra research assistants? In other words, if the staff members are going to get into the game, they need to know where the boundaries are.

Review Progress Periodically

Managers sometimes get nervous when a deadline from a higher-up approaches and they haven't seen a first draft of a major report. For both your peace of mind and the writer's, don't wait until a deadline is too close to meet before you attempt to discover how far along the project is. Set up interim check-back dates throughout the project: When do you want a brief phone call on the sampling selections? When do you want to see a rough draft of the explanation of test results? When do you want to review the entire report or manual outline? Make the writer aware of these periodic deadlines and adhere to them yourself.

26

Obstacles to "Getting It Right the First Time"

A writer should have a willingness to learn; a manager should have a willingness to instruct. They both must respect each other's sensitivities during the editing process.

"I wish I could send up just one report without having it sent back for a rehash." That's not an uncommon sentiment among technical professionals. Even though they share the same objectives, these writers and their bosses often become antagonistic toward each other during the writing project. But with the right approach and attitude, both technical professionals and managers can make their writing projects effective joint ventures.

The Writer's Part

Keep an open mind. People get very defensive about their writing, almost as much as about their appearance or their address. But even novelists and other professional authors have editors and copy assistants who question their work and ask for revisions. Although you never want to submit a document that is less than your best, you may do so inadvertently. When that happens, keep in mind that you're no different from the best professional writers in the world, who frequently find ways to improve their writing when others give them constructive feedback.

Overcome the fear to ask questions when you begin a writing project. Don't assume that you're supposed to know what it is senior management wants to see in a particular report, manual, or proposal. Remember that managers have their own pressures, and with good communication you may be able to put just the slant on your work that will solve both your problems and those of the manager.

You need to have some basic information before you begin to write. Who are the primary readers? Are there hidden audiences? For what purpose is the document being written? Why will readers be interested in what you have to say? Are you simply giving information or making a recommendation? What resources do you have to work with? What are your deadlines? What interim help is your manager willing to give? How will you know if the writing project is successful?

Accept criticism in good faith. Until proven otherwise, assume the manager's motive is simply to turn out a good document. Put yourself in the boss's place and imagine having to affix a signature of approval to someone else's work that you may consider inadequate. That's like sitting on your hands in the middle of a hail storm.

Study the reasons behind suggestions and changes. Simply to review changes made in a particular report has limited value. To understand *why* the changes have been made or requested is a worthwhile pursuit that will gradually enable you to prepare documents in acceptable form on the first attempt.

Compare your first draft to the revised, approved draft; then ask questions about the particular changes. Finally, use the answers to develop broad generalizations about techniques and approaches that will be applicable to subsequent assignments. Verify with the boss that you understand the reasons for the changes and identify which are specific to the project at hand and which should be applied to all writing tasks.

Get other opinions. Don't hesitate to ask colleagues to read your first draft (or quickly review an outline) and make suggestions. The fact that you may be as good a writer as they are is beside the point. Almost any fresh, objective opinion can give you insight into improvements before preparing the final document.

Take responsibility for your own self-improvement. If your writings are frequently revised or returned to you with suggestions for changes, assume that you need to improve your skills generally. Locate a book, a public seminar, or an in-house training course that will provide help.

The Manager's Part

Be understanding about a writer's fear of asking questions. No one can write a totally effective document without having some questions answered about audience and purpose. Managers often assume answers to these questions are obvious; they are not. Remember that subordinates hesitate to ask questions for fear of appearing incompetent. In other words, they often feel as though they should already know the background of a particular situation or that it's their responsibility to "ask around" for further information and suggestions on the proper approach.

Therefore, verify that the writer has indeed understood the writing task *before* he or she spends wasted time writing a misconceived document and you as manager spend wasted time critiquing, asking for a rewrite, and then rereading.

Use a "we're in this together" approach. To overcome a writer's defensive attitude when you are suggesting revisions, use statements such as these: "As far as I understand Big Boss, she wants us to . . . ." "Let's see what we can do by adding such-and-such a point to the executive summary." "How do you think they would react if we went so far as to recommend that . . . ?" "Could we use a circle graph here to show . . . ?"

Offer constructive and specific criticism. Vague generalizations such as "This is just too wordy, Joe" or "This just isn't the approach I had in mind" will do nothing but frustrate the writer and ensure numerous rewrites. Be specific about your suggestions.

Not:

This testing procedure section seems too long.

But:

I think we could cut the XYZ details in this testing procedure section.

Not:

You need to emphasize our credentials in this proposal.

But:

In the credentials section of this proposal, why don't you mention the Benton project we just completed?

Not:

The writing seems a little limp.

But:

Active verbs will be more effective here than passive verbs.

Trying to revise one's writing without specific suggestions is like being told to build a bridge without knowing where.

Lead writers to critique their own work by asking questions rather than only giving flat statements of criticism. Suggestions are much more palatable than judgmental observations. For example, "Do you think a bulleted list would be more effective here than these long paragraphs?" "Can you break this section up with some informative headings?" "Don't you think this is a key point that should be emphasized in the summary?" (If you are one of those unfortunate managers with a stubborn subordinate who would answer no, no, and no to those questions, you may need to consider a more direct approach.)

Find something good to say. You can compliment the writer on the anticipated impact of the paper's conclusions or comment on parts of the writing that are acceptable. There's always something to praise, even if you must say something general, such as "Your sentences are nice and short—easy to read" or "Your test results are impressive."

Leave the responsibility for rewriting to the writer. After you've taken time to make specific suggestions for improvements on several projects, you can begin to turn more and more of the responsibility for revisions over to the writer. Assure the technical professional that you consider effective writing to be a vital part of his or her job. Comment on writing skills and needed improvements in performance appraisals. Help the writer understand that the research task is incomplete without adequate documentation. In other words, emphasize that writing *is* a key part of the work project, not an afterthought.

Allow ownership of good work—and poor. Allow your technical professionals to "own" their work by permitting them to sign their own reports. If your approval is necessary before a document is passed on to a higher-level manager, add your signature line at the bottom of the title page or jointly sign the transmittal letter or memo. Writers find it difficult to pour their heart into a project for which they'll get little recognition.

Likewise, pass on both positive and negative comments from higher-ups about the writing. Writers benefit from that extra feedback and recognition of their contributions.

Show a willingness to invest money in training. If the writer needs more help than you can or want to give, suggest training that will meet the need—a book, a public seminar, or an in-house course. Your willingness to pay for such training sends several messages to the writer: (1) that you are serious about expected improvements, (2) that your suggestions are not just whimsical but are based on principles all technical writers should know, (3) that you consider the writer valuable enough as an employee to invest money and time in training him or her, and (4) that the responsibility for producing effective writing is ultimately the writer's.

Appendixes

Appendix A

Abbreviations and Acronyms

1. Do not use periods with acronyms.

    Not: N.E.C.   *But:* NEC

    Not: O.P.E.C.   *But:* OPEC

2. Use either uppercase or lowercase letters in acronyms, depending on how the word or phrase it represents is written.

    USAR (United States Army Reserve)

    etc. (et cetera)

    mph (miles per hour)

    psi (pounds per square inch)

3. When using both the acronym and the full designation, place the most familiar term outside the parentheses. If the terms are equally familiar, put the acronym inside the parentheses.

    IBM (International Business Machines)

    Prorate Next Command (PN)

4. Use standard technical abbreviations.

    Not: lbs.   *But:* lb

    Not: sec. (second)   *But:* s

Appendix B

Apostrophes

1. To form possession in a singular noun, add an apostrophe and an *s*.

   well's cover   driver's position   operator's input

2. To form possession in a plural noun that ends with a letter other than *s*, add an apostrophe and an *s*.

   women's safety regulations   children's instructions

3. Add an apostrophe to plural nouns ending with *s*. (If an extra syllable is pronounced with the possessive in either the singular, or the plural, you may also add another *s* after the apostrophe.)

   workers' ineligibility   managers' priorities

   Also correct: boss's   bosses' style

4. If a possessive normally would modify another noun, but that noun has been omitted, retain the possessive form.

   The decision to cap the well was John Wiseman's.

5. Don't carelessly place apostrophes in the middle of a possessive word or use an apostrophe when you intend to form a simple plural.

   Not: chassi's condition   two bulldozer's

   But: chassis' condition   two bulldozers

6. Show joint ownership by adding an apostrophe and an *s* only on the last name.

   Howard and Johnson's work   (one research project)

Howard's and Johnson's work   (two research projects)

7. Add an apostrophe and an *s* to express duration.

ten years' experience   a quarter's budget

8. Use an apostrophe to indicate missing letters or numbers.

the new '91 models   can't

9. Use an apostrophe to show the plural of abbreviations, acronyms, numbers, and letters used as words if clarity dictates.

The c's in the user manual are overlapping characters.

The 126's (also 126s) are out of stock.

Let clarity be your guide:

We have plans to redesign the model 234ds.

(Note: It is unclear if the model number is 234d or 234ds. An apostrophe would make clear that the *s* represents the plural form and is not part of the model number.)

We have plans to redesign the model 234d's.

10. Distinguish between modifiers that are intended to be descriptive and modifiers intended to show possession.

the operators manual   (descriptive)
the operator's manual   (possession)
the client meeting   (descriptive)
the client's meeting   (possession)
the competitor bid   (descriptive)
the competitor's bid   (possession)
the Exxon contract   (descriptive)
Exxon's contract   (possession)

Appendix C

Hyphenation

1. Hyphenate the prefixes *ex-, quasi-, self-, all-* and the suffix *-elect*.

   ex-official   quasi-public   self-hypnotist
   all-around   all-encompassing   alderman-elect

2. In the case of almost every other prefix and suffix, write it and the root together as one word.

   nonessential   updated   reinvestigate
   spherelike   fourfold   subcutaneous
   interracial   intravenous   presampling
   contrariwise   pseudointellectual   threesome

3. Use a hyphen between a prefix and a root if necessary to prevent misreading.

   re-cover (to cover again)   recover (to locate)

4. Hyphenate a prefix if the root is capitalized.

   mid-September   non-Jewish

5. Hyphenate two adjectives used as a unit preceding a noun. When the adjectives follow a noun, do not hyphenate them unless they are in altered or inverted form.

   reduced-to-pole map   three-phase plan   10-inch strips
   But: The plan has three phases.

   Note: Do not hyphenate two related adjectives used as a single unit if the two adjectives represent a single concept and are *clearly* recognizable without hyphens.

The hydrogen peroxide solution has fully reacted.

The royalty account statements are complete.

The rental car agency sent a bill.

6. Do not hyphenate adverb-adjective combinations that precede a noun if the adverb ends in *ly*.

   highly publicized campaign   largely ignored plan

   But: well-considered alternative
            less-costly approach

7. Use a suspended hyphen after each prefix or word in a series that modifies the same term.

   The pre- and postgraduate work has been considered.

   The three- and four-tier platforms have been moved.

8. Hyphenate compound numbers from twenty-one to ninety-nine.

   forty-four   eighty-two

9. Hyphenate compound words without a noun as their base when the compound is used as a noun.

   go-between   follow-through   higher-up

Appendix D

Capitalization

1. Capitalize the name of specific places or regions.
   Colorado   Dallas   the Mediterranean   the South
2. Do not capitalize directions.
   Move toward the southwestern part of the region.
   He reported that he was traveling south on I35.
3. Capitalize races and languages.
   Jewish   Caucasian   Malaysian   French
4. Capitalize days of the week, months, and special days, but not seasons of the year.
   Wednesday   July   Hanukkah   winter   fall
5. Capitalize historical periods and events.
   the Fifties   the Dark Ages
   the Industrial Revolution
6. Capitalize trade names, company names, organizations, divisions, and agencies.

Southwestern Bell	Scotch Guard
Plexiglas	Air Traffic Control
Xerox	Elavil
Region 7 Marketing Division	Internal Revenue Service

7. Do not capitalize generic words such as the following unless they are used as part of an official name.

251

our manufacturing group	Buford Manufacturing Inc.
the engineering budget	Engineering and Quality Control
to the agency	Herman Regulatory Agency
forward to the company	Exxon Company USA
the federal government	Federal Deposit Insurance Corporation

8. Capitalize the title of a corporate position only when it precedes a name and is used as a person's title. Do not capitalize the position title when it follows or replaces an individual's name. Do not capitalize a generic reference to a position or organization (unless your own corporation's style book mandates such capitalization).

   Mary Smith, director of research, has approved the budget.

   Director of Research Mary Smith has approved the budget.

   Our board of directors has made the decision.

   Our Board of Directors has made the decision.

   Four company officials have resigned.

9. Capitalize the first word of a direct quotation except when the quotation continues rather than begins a sentence.

   Our proposal claims, "Amherst will not initiate legal proceedings against Bilco Inc."

   The research plan calls for "exhaustive and detailed" analysis of the problem.

10. Capitalize the first word of an independent question within a sentence. You are also correct to use lowercase.

    The determining factor is, Will we reimburse them for the charges?

    The determining factor is, will we . . .

11. Capitalize the first word of items in a formal list. (It is also acceptable not to capitalize items when the items are not complete sentences. It is also acceptable not to capitalize items when the items are syntactically connected to the introducing clause or phrase.)

The criteria are:	The criteria are
• Experience in dredging	• experience in dredging
• Equipment on site	• equipment on site
• Budgetary provisions	• budgetary provisions

12. Capitalize the first word and all principal words in a heading or title. Do not capitalize prepositions, conjunctions, or articles unless they are the first or last words of a title.

    Fundamentals of Petroleum by Daniel T. Ortega

    Quantal Release of Transmitter Is Not Associated with Channel Opening on the Neuronal Membrane

13. Capitalize a term derived from a proper noun unless it is so familiar that it is no longer associated with the original name.

    Eschka's Mixture

    Newton's Second Law

    Parkinson's Law

    But: aspirin   hertz   ohm   volt

Index

Note: Figure references are listed in italics.